THE LIFE CYCLE SERIES

Understanding Stress and Anxiety

Charles Spielberger

HARPER & ROW, PUBLISHERS

New York   Hagerstown   Philadelphia

San Francisco   London   Sydney

This book was devised and produced
by Multimedia Publications Inc

General Editor: *Dr. Leonard Kristal*
Prod Mgr/Art Dir/Design: *Bob Vari*
Picture Researcher: *Judy Kristal*

First published in Holland 1979 by
Multimedia Publications Inc

British Library Cataloguing in Publication Data
Spielberger, Charles
    Understanding Stress and Anxiety
    References pg. 118–121
    Includes index
ISBN 06 384747 7 paper

Colour origination: United Artists Ltd, Israel
Typeset by CCC and printed and bound by William Clowes & Sons Limited
Beccles and London

Contents

I Stress and strain

Coping with stress and anxiety is an every-day requirement for normal human growth and development. Going to school, or into a new job, for the first time, being separated from parents or loved ones, doubting one's own adequacy in relations with other people, job pressures and deadlines, speaking or entertaining in public are among the many potential sources of stress.

Stress is an integral part of the natural fabric of life. Any situation in which a person's behaviour is evaluated by others can be stressful. While stress may have positive as well as negative effects, the negative aspects generally get the most attention. For example, stress is widely regarded as the cause of such diverse unpleasantness as bad putting on the golf course, poor performance in examinations, insomnia, headaches, skin rashes, and even serious medical disorders like stomach ulcers, heart attacks and cancer.

In commonsense terms, stress refers both to the circumstances that place physical or psychological demands on an individual and to the emotional reactions experienced in these situations. Going to the dentist, taking a test, or applying for a job are generally considered to be stressful life events. Most people feel nervous and uncomfortable in the reception room as they await their turn in the dentist's chair. Many students experience rapid heartbeat and dryness in the mouth as the questions for an examination are being passed out. An applicant for a new position may become upset and nauseous immediately before the job interview. Even crossing a busy street or making an important telephone call can cause a person to feel tense and apprehensive.

The adverse effects of stress on physical health and emotional well-being are increasingly recognised. But there is as yet little agreement among experts on the definition of stress. One of the world's foremost medical authorities on the effects of stress on bodily processes is Dr Hans Selye. In his popular book, *Stress Without Distress*, Selye asks 'What is Stress?' and then gives this answer:

> Everybody has it, everybody talks about it, yet few people have taken the trouble to find out what stress really is. . . . Nowadays we hear a great deal at social gatherings about the stress of executive life, retirement, exercise, family problems, pollution, air traffic control or the death of a relative. . . . The word

The kind of stress that everybody enjoys—watchers as well as players; but for professional sportsmen other pressures may not be so pleasant.

'stress', like 'success', 'failure', or 'happiness', means different things to different people so that defining it is extremely difficult.

The business man who is under constant pressure from his clients and employees alike, the air traffic controller who knows that a moment of distraction may mean death to hundreds of people, the athlete who wants to win a race and the husband who helplessly watches as his wife slowly and painfully dies of cancer all suffer from stress. The problems they face are totally different, but medical research has shown that in many respects the body responds in a stereotyped manner, with identical biochemical changes, essentially meant to cope with any type of increased demand upon the human machinery.[1]

From Selye's analysis, it is apparent that stress affects many aspects of life, and that coping with stress is essential for physical health and effective performance. But how do we cope with something that appears to be so elusive and difficult to define?

Cornered! A classic instigator of high tension in the victim.

In order to understand stress, we must have a clear conception of the nature of anxiety and how it is related to stress. Anxiety encompasses tension, nervousness, fear and worry. This unpleasant emotion has a pervasive influence on contemporary life that can be seen in literature, the arts, religion, and in many other facets of our culture. Consider, for example, the following passage from *Time* magazine:

> Anxiety seems to be the dominant fact . . . and is threatening to become the dominant cliché . . . of modern life. It shouts in the headlines, laughs nervously at cocktail parties, nags from advertisements, speaks suavely in the board room, whines from the stage, clatters from the Wall Street ticker, jokes with fake youthfulness on the golf course and whispers in privacy each day before the shaving mirror and the dressing table. Not merely the black statistics of murder, suicide, alcoholism and divorce betray anxiety (or that special form of anxiety which is guilt), but almost any innocent, everyday act: the limp or overhearty handshake, the second pack of cigarettes or the third Martini, the forgotten appointment, the stammer in mid-sentence, the wasted hour before the TV set, the spanked child, the new car unpaid for.[2]

These passages reflect considerable overlap in the meaning of 'stress' and 'anxiety', and suggest that the terms are used interchangeably by both scientists and laymen. Stress and anxiety are also, obviously, enormously popular topics of conversation—naturally enough, since they refer to situations and experiences that directly affect people's lives. As will be noted later in this book, numerous techniques have been developed for reducing stress and anxiety, ranging from yoga and Transcendental Meditation to the prescription of ocean cruises, a change of scene and tranquillising drugs.

Yoga and relaxation exercises can relieve stress—unless you get anxious about doing them right!

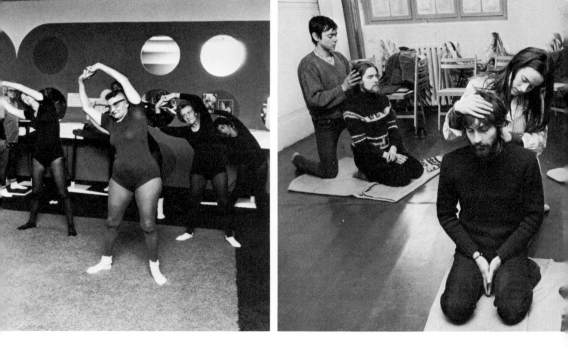

Stress and strain

Breeding-ground for uncontrolled stresses on city dwellers . . .

. . . and where everything depends on precisely controlled tensions.

The term 'stress', of Latin derivation, was first used in English during the 17th century to describe distress, oppression, hardship and adversity. During the 18th and 19th centuries, the popular meaning of stress shifted to denote a force, pressure or strong influence acting upon a physical object or person. This definition carried with it the connotation that an external force induced a 'strain' in an object which attempted to maintain its integrity by resisting the distorting power of this force. In popular usage, that is to say, stress *causes* strain—a proposition that can be written in the form:

Stress → Strain

The concept of stress was introduced into the physical sciences in a manner that served to reinforce the popular usage. In early investigations of the elastic properties of solid materials, 'stress' referred to external pressure or force applied to an object, while 'strain' denoted the resulting internal distortion or change in the object's size or shape.[3] In physics and engineering the relationships between stress and strain can be quantitatively expressed (in lb/sq. in. or kg/sq. cm., for example) by measuring the force acting on a unit area of the material. This relationship depends upon the molecular structure of the material, and defines the resilience of the material to the forces acting upon it.

A simple example will illustrate these concepts. If a weight is attached to the end of a rope, the rope will stretch. The degree to which it stretches will be proportional to the weight that is

applied. The effect of the weight is to create an internal force within the rope that causes it to stretch, and, eventually, break. Current engineering terminology defines the external force as the *load*; the internal force is called *stress*, and the stretching and eventual breaking of the rope is called *strain*.

In building a bridge or a skyscraper, or designing a wing for a jet aircraft, it is essential to know how much stress will be exerted by a specified load so that the amount of strain that the material can withstand without breaking can be calculated. Building codes generally specify a large 'safety' factor which ensures that construction materials will meet specified standards.

Speculation about the effects of life stress on physical and mental illness began in the 19th century. In the early 20th century, Sir William Osler, a renowned British physician, equated 'stress and strain' with 'hard work and worry', and suggested that these conditions contributed to the development of heart disease.[4] In commenting on the personal attributes of a group of 20 medical doctors suffering from *angina pectoris* (a heart disorder in which the patient experiences intense chest pains), Osler observed that these physicians were completely absorbed with 'the incessant treadmill of the practice of medicine, and in every one of these men there was an added factor—worry'.

In equating stress with hard work and strain with worry, Osler has applied definitions used in physics and engineering to problems of human adjustment and behaviour. Clearly, doctors dedicated to serving the needs of their patients encounter a great deal of pressure and it is not surprising that this produces worry and anxiety reactions. If the pressure persists, then serious medical problems such as heart disease or an ulcer can result for the doctor himself.

But people are considerably more complex than inorganic

Among stressful jobs, few are more onerous or cause more strain than the air traffic controller's.

materials; they have the ability to anticipate the future, and to interact with and change the environment. Consequently, whether or not a stressful situation arouses an anxiety reaction depends on how a person sees or interprets that situation, and on the individual's 'coping skills'. Thus, some people react to hard work and responsibility with worry and anxiety while the same amount and type of work can be challenging and rewarding for others. Let us analyse several rather simple situations that most people perceive as stressful in order to illustrate the concepts here discussed—stress, strain, emotional reaction and adjustment.

Sharp-toothed sorrow . . .

'You won't feel a thing . . .' but already his feelings are of acute distress at just being there.

Imagine a four-year-old visiting a dental surgery for the first time. His mother has told him it will only be a 'check-up' examination that will not hurt him. He is very cheerful as he enters the waiting room and takes a seat beside his mother, and is given a colouring book to occupy his attention. But he

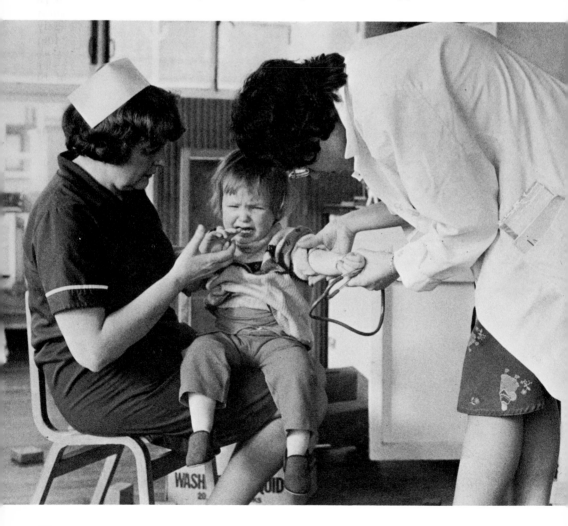

nevertheless notices an unfamiliar 'medicine' smell and strange noises coming from the dentist's surgery; and one of the other children in the waiting room is crying and pleading with his mother to go home.

The boy becomes restless and reaches out to grasp his mother's hand. His eyes are tearful as he remembers what his mother said before leaving home: 'big boys' are not frightened by the dentist. He also recalls being teased by his older brother, who vividly described how much it hurt when the dentist stuck a big needle in his mouth and used a drill to remove the decay before filling a cavity. These thoughts are very clear in his mind. He is comforted by his mother's reassurance, but becomes increasingly restless and apprehensive as he waits his turn to see the dentist.

When his name is finally called by the nurse, he is frightened and begins to cry, refusing to enter the dentist's office. He turns to his mother and begs her to go home. After further reassurances from his mother, and from the dentist (who is kindly and understanding), he eventually agrees to the examination—but only on condition that his mother remains with him.

Parents and children are familiar with the stress of dental treatment; nearly everyone has experienced anxiety about going to the dentist. Indeed, many adults who were traumatised during childhood by painful, unpleasant experiences associated with dental treatment postpone or avoid dental examinations until serious problems arise.

Examination, test, ordeal?

Consider the case of a young woman for whom a forthcoming examination will be an important factor in her selection for admission to university. She has excellent grades; her friends and teachers have told her that she will have no difficulty in being accepted at the college of her choice. Yet, despite her ability and academic achievement, she knows she will experience intense feelings of tension, apprehension and nervousness when she takes the examination. On similar occasions in the past, she has suffered from physical symptoms like trembling, heart palpitation, nausea and dizziness during tests.

In order to compensate for her test anxiety, she spends a great deal of time and effort in preparation for examinations. She has good study habits and sets aside a special time each day to work on her lessons. Nevertheless, even though she is usually well prepared, taking tests is a painful experience that affects her mentally as well as physically.

Before the big examination, she reviews the materials recommended by her teacher and has little difficulty in answering the practice questions that were distributed in advance to help students prepare for it. On the day of the examination, she arrives early and takes a seat near the front of the classroom. As the papers are being passed out, she begins to tremble, and feels nauseous and dizzy. She cannot forget how important her performance on this test is to her future plans.

11

For how many of them will true ability go unrecognised because of 'examination nerves'?

Trying to answer the first few test items, her mind seems to go blank. This is especially distressing because she is certain that she knows the answers. Thoughts of doing poorly, of not being admitted to university, and of the disappointment that she and her parents will feel, keep crossing her mind. There is a time limit and she is keenly aware of the movement of the hands of the clock. She is wasting valuable time, and the pressure and tension continue to mount as she works. Her anxiety and worry clearly distract her attention from the task at hand.

Although there is no physical pain in prospect, taking an examination is as stressful for this girl as the child's dental checkup is for him. Apprehension about taking a test that will have an important bearing on her future, and the unpleasant experience of actually working on the test, produce a great deal of emotional pain. Even though she may perform better than average on the college entrance examination, her scores are lower than would be predicted on the basis of her high ability.

For some people, the stress associated with taking tests produces intense anxiety, which can have negative immediate effects as well as far-reaching long-term consequences. Examination stress, test anxiety and academic achievement will be considered in greater detail in a later chapter.

Afflictions of the applicant

Our third parable concerns a young man—an immigrant—whose interest in motor cars began when he was a child. He has fond memories of helping his father repair the family car; and he greatly enjoyed working on his own jalopy. After attending a technical high school, he is taking a six-month course in car mechanics that will soon be completed. It is now time for him to find a suitable job in which he can use his new knowledge and skills to earn a living.

Although he did well in the auto mechanics course, this young man had a lot of difficulty in high school, especially in subjects that needed English language and reading skills. His mother tongue is not English, and he has always felt insecure and embarrassed when called upon to recite in class, where most of the other students were native-born English speakers.

On the basis of his excellent performance in the auto mechanics course, he has been highly recommended by his instructors for a job at a garage in a town near-by. But as the time for the job interview approaches he begins to feel restless, tense and very self-conscious, and begins to wonder whether he can make a good enough impression on his potential employer to get the job.

On the day of his interview he feels even worse: he has not slept well the night before, and has taken several aspirins to relieve a headache that has persisted all morning. He loves to work on cars and is confident of his ability to apply the knowledge

Applying mechanical knowledge in an underhand way ...

and skills he has recently learned, but the interview fills him with apprehension. Feeling sick, he has to fight down an impulse to leave the waiting room.

In the manager's office at last, his knees tremble and his mouth is dry. His mind seems foggy, and his answers to the manager's questions are slow and stilted. His performance does not do him justice. Were it not for the fact that the manager knows and trusts the young man's instructors, he would not have been offered the chance to prove his real worth on the job.

Applying for a job is stressful because it involves being examined and judged by other people. While such evaluations are obviously not physically dangerous or painful, they *are* psychologically threatening, because no one likes to be rebuffed or rejected. Indeed, most people are deeply concerned about what others think of them. Thus, we experience tension and anxiety when we are faced with a personal evaluation, and are likely to feel embarrassed and disappointed when we do poorly in situations such as applying for a job or seeking admission to a social club or professional organisation.

Defining stress and anxiety

Going to the dentist, taking a test, and applying for a job are examples of situations that are usually regarded as potentially damaging, either physically or psychologically. At first glance, it may seem that the feelings of apprehension, emotional tension and worry experienced by people in these situations stem directly from the possibility of harm inherent in them. On closer examination, however, it is apparent that emotional reactions to stressful situations are influenced by both the *real* potential dangers of these situations and individual assessments of the situations.

There was no real pain involved in the child's dental check-up, certainly not in the waiting room. However, the cues of the situation—the 'medicine smells', strange noises and crying child—caused him to interpret the situation as potentially dangerous, and he became fearful. Had the girl known for sure that she would be admitted to college regardless of her scores on the entrance examination, she would probably have seen her examination as no more stressful than the practice questions with which she had had little difficulty. Similarly, the young man's anxiety about applying for a job was related more to his fear of being rejected because of his difficulty in expressing himself than to the real problems presented in the course of the job interview.

Reactions to stressful situations are based on individual appraisals and interpretations; nevertheless some situations are inherently more stressful than others. The mother's need to reassure her child that the dentist would not hurt him reflects a

fear of dental treatment that is nearly universal. The girl's apprehension about an examination that would have an important bearing on her future is widely—and realistically—shared by almost all other candidates in important examinations. And while the motor mechanic's language difficulties undoubtedly contributed to his intense emotional reaction to the job interview, almost everyone experiences some anxiety in situations in which they are evaluated by others.

When people interpret a stressful situation as dangerous or threatening, they experience feelings of tension, apprehension and worry. They also undergo a range of physiological and behavioural changes resulting from the activation or arousal of the autonomic nervous system.[5] The *intensity* of the reaction is proportional to the magnitude of the *perceived* danger or threat.

Feelings of tension, apprehension, nervousness and worry—as well as behavioural and physiological changes such as trembling, heart palpitations and dizziness—are often symptoms of anxiety.[6] Before his dental examination, the boy became increasingly apprehensive, restless and tearful in the waiting room; as the question papers for the college entrance examination were being passed out, the girl began to tremble and perspire, and felt nauseous and dizzy; the young man had difficulty sleeping the night before his job interview and woke the next morning with a headache that persisted all day, and when he entered the garage manager's office he felt a 'knot' in his stomach, his heart was beating rapidly, and his throat was dry.

Moments of anxiety for passengers and crew; and rather more prolonged stress for those living underneath them.

Working at the far edge of your talents and abilities is stressful— but also immensely satisfying.

If we now refer back to the analogy with the physical sciences, we can see that *situations* like those we have described can be roughly equated with *stress*, and *anxiety* with *strain*. But while there is general agreement that stress causes strain (or anxiety), these concepts refer to and emphasise different aspects of a complex psychobiological process, and the boundary between them is unclear. We have therefore to go further in splitting the processes involved so as to define our terms carefully. (And we are not going to be helped by the fact that a variety of other terms such as pressure, conflict, tension, emotion, nervousness and worry may all be used to describe similar phenomena.)

In this volume, the term *stress* will be used to refer to a complex psychobiological process that consists of three major elements.[7] The process is *initiated* by a situation or stimulus that is potentially harmful or dangerous (*stressor*). If a stressor is *interpreted* as dangerous or threatening, an *anxiety reaction* will be elicited. Thus, our working definition of stress refers to the following temporal sequence of events:

Stressor → **Perception of threat** → **Anxiety state**

The term *stressor* will be used in this book to describe situations or stimuli that are objectively characterised by some degree of physical or psychological danger. The term *threat* refers to the individual's perception or appraisal of that situation or stimulus as potentially dangerous or harmful.[8] People who see a stressful situation as threatening will experience an anxiety reaction. The term *state anxiety* will be used in this book to describe an emotional reaction that consists of subjective feelings of tension, apprehension, nervousness and worry, and heightened activity of the autonomic nervous system. The overall process is referred to as *stress*.

The nature of stressors and various common sources of stress are described in Chapter 2 of this book. The relationship between stress, threat and anxiety is considered in Chapter 3. In Chapter 4, the distinction is made between fear and objective and neurotic anxiety, and we examine the difference between anxiety as a transitory emotional state (state anxiety) and as a personality characteristic (trait anxiety).

The relationship between stress, state and trait anxiety and adjustment are considered in Chapter 5; there we also look at psychological mechanisms for reducing anxiety states and at some questionnaires for measuring state and trait anxiety. Chapter 6 discusses examination stress, the effects of anxiety on academic achievement, and worry and emotion in test situations. In Chapter 7, methods commonly used for minimising stress and reducing state anxiety are examined; and therapeutic approaches for the treatment of anxiety are considered. In the final chapter, we suggest some general principles and guidelines that may help *you* to cope more effectively with stress and anxiety.

2 Sources of stress

Stressful circumstances are encountered every day and at every stage of human development. There is even evidence that stress before birth can influence both the mother and the fetus and that it may contribute to obstetric complications and birth defects. From the trauma of birth itself right through to adolescence, the young meet unavoidable sources of stress: from weaning and toilet training as babies to the process of formal education and learning social skills a little later.

Young adults are confronted with the difficult task of choosing a career and finding a job. Pressures at work and from the social groups to which we belong, stresses inherent in marriage and family relationships must be contended with throughout life. Retirement and old age are not only states or stages of life but themselves among the ubiquitous sources of stress.

Hurricanes, floods and wars are examples of catastrophic stressors that exert exceptional pressures on large masses of people. Adverse weather conditions such as droughts and sudden unseasonal frosts can be especially stressful for farmers while city dwellers must bear crowded living conditions, street crime, noise and pollution. Even holidays, usually regarded as periods of relaxation or at least as positive events, are extremely stressful for some people.

This chapter examines sources of stress that are encountered during the normal course of human growth and development. We also look at stressors in our surroundings such as crowding, traffic congestion and the noise of city life. Clearly, a particular stressor may affect different people in different ways; but it is interesting that people from different cultures see much the same degree of danger in many stressful events. The last section of this chapter shows how surprisingly little culture matters in that particular respect.

Stress and human development

For some time doctors and laymen have recognised the potentially traumatic effects of stress during pregnancy and labour.[1] Not only the mother but also the fetus and the new-born infant can be affected: during the past quarter-century animal experiments have shown bad effects on the mother and the fetus, which may even lead to birth defects.[2, 3]

Faces in the crowd bear the characteristic expression of urban dwellers oppressed by their own numbers.

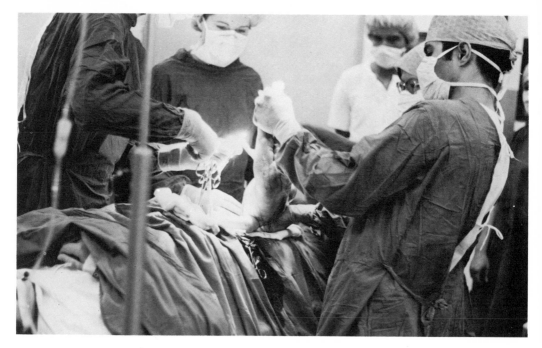

The trauma of birth, magnified in this case (for mother and child) by caesarean section.

Research with humans confirms these findings. Two recent studies found that different patterns of anxiety during pregnancy were associated with obstetric complications. In one, women who reported higher levels of anxiety during the first three months of pregnancy experienced more obstetric complications than women with problem-free pregnancies.[4] The other found that anxiety was higher during the seven weeks before delivery for women who experienced obstetric complications.[5] This research gives new urgency to the search for ways of minimising the adverse impact of stress and anxiety on human reproduction.

The arrival of a new baby is a potential source of stress for the entire family. The extreme helplessness of the infant means the mother must make many changes in her daily life and give up much of her autonomy and freedom. She must also teach the infant to modify or delay the immediate gratification of its needs so that taking care of him does not wholly disrupt the life of the family. In feeding and caring for the baby, a mother has less time to spend with other members of the family, and this can be stressful for her husband and other children.

For many decades now, mainstream psychoanalysis has maintained that the way in which the stresses of infancy and childhood are handled can have profound effects on subsequent personality development. Some psychoanalysts believe, for example, that a baby who is fed every time he cries, whether or not he is hungry, can become a rather passive and dependent person later in life. On the other hand, it seems that if gratification of a child's needs for food and sucking are too much delayed, he can grow up to be suspicious, mistrustful or demanding.

You can drive your child 'potty'...

Toilet training is a matter of considerable concern for many parents and a universal source of stress for the young child. During the first year of life, relatively few demands are made on the child. Therefore, when toilet training begins in the second or third year, a child can be overwhelmed by parental pressure to control the biological functions of his bladder and bowels. If toilet training begins too early, the child will be physically unable to comply with his parent's wishes; and excessively punitive toilet training procedures generally evoke intense feelings of anxiety. Harvard psychologist Jerome Kagan has identified five long-term psychological consequences of severe toilet training:[6] anger at and fear of the trainer, usually the mother; anxiety about the genital organs which may contribute to adult sexual conflicts; anxiety over being 'dirty'; feelings of insecurity and inadequacy; and a lack of curiosity and spontaneity in behaviour.

Between the tenth and eighteenth month of life, most children spontaneously begin to speak. The early speech of young children is characterised by frequent pauses, the repetition of sounds, and the mispronunciation of words. These nonfluencies are normal and tend to disappear as the child's speaking skills develop with practice. However, learning to speak fluently takes place over a long period of time, and this process can be very stressful if parents put too much pressure on the young child to speak clearly and precisely. Indeed, a child may develop stuttering if his parents' criticism makes him feel self-conscious and anxious about speaking.

The initial stresses of toilet training are obviously a thing of the past for these children

Stressful school environments

Going to school normally marks the first continuous separation of a child from its parents. The school is also the first socialising agent outside the family that is encountered by most children. While good teachers provide assistance and emotional support for the child, they are also sources of stress when they need to correct mistakes or punish misbehaviour. Since the child must learn many new and difficult tasks on which there is a risk of failure, the manner in which a teacher corrects and disciplines the child is especially important.

Getting along, and feeling secure and comfortable, with teachers and other pupils is an essential foundation for future learning. Nursery schools and kindergartens provide opportunities for children to learn to adapt to school environments under conditions that are less stressful than those usually found in regular school classes. The emphasis in these settings is on the social and emotional adjustment of the child in an informal atmosphere.

Learning to read is generally the first stressful educational task that confronts the school child. By six years of age, most children

The happiest days of their lives ... but in spite of, or because of, the high pressures associated with modern education?

have developed the physical, intellectual and language skills that are required in reading. However, some children are much better prepared than others because more attention was given at home to developing their language and communications skills.

The stresses associated with learning to read were reflected in a recent American study of first graders who differed in reading readiness.[7] Children who came to school with a low reading readiness developed more anxiety in responding to school demands than did children who were higher in reading readiness at the beginning of the year. Thus, as might be expected, the amount of anxiety associated with learning to read is much greater for children who are not well prepared when they first enter school.

The 'open classroom' and individualised self-paced instruction are examples of new educational techniques that try to reduce educational stress. In 'open classrooms', children generally work in small groups, and there is less structure and routine than in traditional classes. A child's maturity and readiness to learn, rather than his chronological age, are used to decide the work he is given. This makes it possible for each child to progress at his own rate, unencumbered by the traditional lock-step method of instruction.

Strict means better?

It has been shown that stress is greater, and the average level of anxiety is higher, in traditional classes than in 'open classrooms'.[8] But it is also true that the level of academic achievement in 'open classrooms' is poorer for some students than it is under traditional systems of instruction. It seems that stress actually helps some students academically—and this may depend on the difficulty of the material to be learned and on the intelligence and personality traits of the student.

Changing schools, transition from primary to secondary school and entry to university are also major sources of stress. In adapting to a new school a student must establish working relationships with a different set of teachers and gain acceptance from classmates. The competition in high school and university is also more intense than in primary school, and the possibility of failure is considerably greater. In seeking entrance to universities, students must compete with each other for admission, and this can be acutely stressful, as exemplified in the case of the young woman candidate described in Chapter 1.

Career and job stress

Job satisfaction, material success and recognition from others are, in general, what even the least ambitious person among us hopes for from the work he or she does. So the task of choosing a career and finding a job in which one can pursue it places great pressure on young people in their twenties. Even when a person clearly knows what he or she would like to do, and has the necessary skills and training to perform well, competing for a job can produce high levels of anxiety, especially in conditions of high general unemployment. The case of the young motor mechanic described in Chapter 1 is nowadays common, at least as far as the degree of stress is concerned.

In today's world, young women are increasingly confronted with a conflict between pursuing a career or opting for the equally demanding role of wife and mother. There are stresses associated with both alternatives, and with choosing between them. Those women who decide single-mindedly to pursue a career must deal with the same pressures encountered by young men. Those who choose to become primarily homemakers are faced with the no less difficult task of selecting the 'right' husband. Needless to say, combining both roles presents an even more stressful alternative.

The penalties of being rational: this proves you should not walk under ladders (but see page 31).

Every job includes many potential sources of stress—poor working conditions, long hours, time pressures and deadlines, and difficult relationships with supervisors and fellow employees may individually or in combination produce deleterious pressures. The same applies to conflicts between vocational and family demands, to the bearing of too much—or too little—responsibility, and to the misuse or underuse of an individual's talents and skills.

In urban societies, there are families which change their residence as often as every year; and among managerial personnel, frequent moves may be accepted as a 'hazard of the job'. One survey of a group of executives revealed that no less than a third of them had relocated every four or five years. In a study of the mobility of 2,000 managers, two-thirds reported that they expected to be transferred every three years or so.[9] Moving from one city to another, or even changing neighbourhoods in the same town, can be especially stressful for wives and children who are faced with adapting to a strange environment and making new friends.

Some jobs are inherently more stressful than others. The test pilot and the soldier in combat must often risk their lives in carrying out their responsibilities. Police officers and air traffic controllers work under demanding conditions in which the safety of others depends on their judgement and skill. The stress affecting police officers in the United States is reflected in a suicide rate more than twice the average for urban males.[10] American air traffic controllers have a much higher than average incidence of diseases known to be induced or aggravated by stress, such as ulcers and hypertension, and the onset of these conditions occurs at an earlier age than in the population at large.[11]

Marriage and aging

A mature well-adjusted spouse can be a constant source of emotional support and a reducer of stress. A sympathetic ear helps us all to understand and cope with our problems better. On the other hand, an incompatible, conflict-ridden relationship between husband and wife can be an unending source of stress. There are more than one million divorces each year in the United States alone, where half of all marriages ultimately end in divorce and many more in separation.

With advancing age, most people become increasingly vulnerable to a wide range of stressors. Inevitable decline in physical capacity may interfere with the ability to continue doing a good job: most professional athletes are forced to retire before the age of 40; many air traffic controllers have 'burn-out' problems in their late thirties which require them to change to less stressful occupations.

There is also much less job mobility and fewer opportunities

for promotion with advancing age. For most people, personal income declines after retirement and this may require a radical readjustment in their standard of living. Physical and psychological disorders increase with age: the incidence of heart disease, cancer, arthritis, and glaucoma increases rapidly after the age of 50. Physiological and psychological changes associated with menopause in women and the decline in sexual capacity in men can arouse intense anxiety. Such changes may also undermine self-respect and mental health, and can lead to the onset of depression so severe that hospital care is needed.

Environmental stress

Sources of stress in our surroundings range from natural and man-made disasters, like earthquakes and wars, to the daily annoyances of commuting to work in heavy traffic or on a crowded train or having to queue in the rain for a bus. The press of people, noise, and air and water pollution are also common sources of life stress in the city.

Many people believe that the pace and pressures of modern civilisation—and hence the stresses—are more severe than they were in the 'good old days'. This may well be so, although the concurrence of the Great Plague and the Great Fire cannot have afforded Londoners, for example, a restful time in 1666: but certainly things are different. These days, the impact of unsettling events around us is intensified by the almost instantaneous communication of news about their occurrence.

People are also now much more aware of and concerned about what goes on in other parts of the world. They realise that remote events can have both immediate and long-term effects on their own lives. The imposition of an oil embargo in the Middle East, for example, can quickly result in long queues at petrol stations in Europe and North America.

A century ago there was much more physical drudgery than there is now, and people were more vulnerable to natural disasters and disease. There were also fewer luxuries. The need for independence and self-reliance was greater in a predominantly rural society in which one's nearest neighbour might live a considerable distance away. In some respects life is easier today: modern labour-saving devices clean our homes, wash our clothes, cook our meals and rapidly transport us from place to place. However, since we depend on these conveniences, we are much more helpless than our forefathers were if for some reason—power failures, strikes, fuel shortages—they are suddenly not available to us.

For the city dweller, crowded living conditions are one of the most obvious and important sources of stress. Noise, traffic congestion, and pollution are among the many by-products of high population density. Unemployment, poverty, malnutrition, and poor sanitary conditions are also still generally associated with large cities. Slums are still with us. During the industrial revolution, crowded living conditions lowered the resistance of

When life's most basic need is not met, environmental stresses go unnoticed

slum-dwellers to infectious diseases and contributed to the rapid spread of, and high mortality from, the scourges of tuberculosis, typhoid, cholera and influenza. In the cities of Europe and North America immunisation, improved sanitary conditions and public health programmes have substantially reduced the occurrence of epidemics of these diseases, but tuberculosis, typhoid and cholera still kill millions of people each year in Africa and Asia.

Like crowding, noise—another chief constituent of urban stress—can have adverse effects on human physiology and behaviour. It has been shown that high intensity noise can damage hearing and lead to an increase in blood pressure. Uncontrollable noise also lowers tolerance to frustration and increases aggressive behaviour; and it reduces performance on complex problem-solving tasks. Moreover, research has shown that the negative effects of noise may persist over long periods of time even after the noise has stopped.

The 'madding crowd' grows daily madder ...

Psychologists David Glass and Jerome Singer investigated the long-term effects of noise on children who lived in a high-rise apartment directly over a busy New York City expressway.[12] They found that children who had lived for four years or more in the noisier lower floors of this building had greater difficulty in discriminating between similar-sounding words (for example, 'cope' and 'coke', 'gear' and 'beer') than children who lived on the quieter upper floors. The children who were exposed to more noise also did worse on tests of reading ability. And this is quite apart from the devastating physiological effects known to follow exposure to very low frequency sound.

Traffic congestion is a constant source of stress for urban commuters who must spend a considerable part of each day travelling between their homes and work. During rush hours, especially, frustration over traffic delays can generate anger and anxiety. It has been shown that even short-term laboratory

exposure to simulated road conditions causes the heart to beat faster and increases perspiration and the secretion of hormones associated with stress reactions. The evidence also suggests that driving a car under stressful conditions may lower driving skills and even contribute to emotional difficulties and less efficient behaviour after the journey is over.[13]

'Well, I did say it wouldn't be a stylish marriage.'

A group of California psychologists confirmed these findings when they investigated changes in mood and behaviour in people who regularly used their cars to commute to work. The results indicated that commuters who travel greater distances or spend more time travelling between work and home reported more concern about traffic congestion and inconvenience, less satisfaction with commuting, and a greater desire to change their residence. People who spent more time and energy in commuting also had higher blood pressure and reported being more annoyed after arrival at work.

Stressful life events

There is substantial evidence that stressful life events play an important role in causing physical and mental illness. There is a clear connection between stress and a number of different diseases, including heart attacks, ulcers, arthritis, allergic reactions, and psychiatric conditions such as anxiety-neurosis and depression. It is important, therefore, to identify specific life events that are especially harmful.

A questionnaire developed by Thomas Holmes and Richard Rahe, *The Social Readjustment Rating Scale* (SRRS), has been

When you are half-way up the ladder of success, children can be a burden.

widely used to investigate the relationship between stressful life events and illness.[14] Their research was based on clinical interviews, medical histories, and a series of studies with more than 5,000 patients. From it they were able to identify 43 life events or changes in life style that were associated with the onset of disease. These included changes in health, family relationships, economic and living conditions, education, religion and social affairs. And they ranged in severity from major life crises like divorce or the death of a spouse to relatively minor annoyances such as a change in diet or receiving a traffic ticket. Positive life changes—for example, an 'outstanding personal achievement' or 'taking a holiday'—were also included.

All the SRRS life events require people to make adjustments in their accustomed pattern of behaviour. Holmes and Rahe assumed that the degree of readjustment required by a particular life event could be taken as an index of the severity of stress. So they asked a diverse group of American men and women to give their opinions as to the amount of change in coping behaviour that would be required to adjust to each event.

In order to provide a framework for rating these life events, marriage was selected as a datum line and given an arbitrary numerical value of 50. The participants in the study were instructed to decide, first, whether a particular life event would require more or less readjustment than marriage, and then to indicate the amount of readjustment they felt would be needed to cope with the event by assigning a number proportionally larger or smaller than 50. *Life change unit* (LCU) scores, defined as the average score for a specific event, were computed for each of the 43 life events.

The table published on page 35 shows the 15 life events which American subjects judged to require the greatest amount of readjustment, with the LCU values assigned to them. Six of these events had LCU values greater than 50, indicating that they were judged to require *more* readjustment than marriage. The remaining 36 life events had LCU values lower than 50, and were thus judged to need *less* readjustment than marriage.

The three life events that were rated as 'most stressful in terms of the amount of readjustment they would entail' were 'death of a spouse', 'divorce', and 'marital separation', with LCU scores of 100, 73, and 65 respectively. The three events rated as requiring the least amount of readjustment were 'minor violations of the law', 'Christmas', and 'holidays', for which the LCU scores ranged from 11 to 13.

The participants in the Holmes–Rahe study were heterogeneous in terms of their age, sex and marital status. Nevertheless, it is interesting to note that agreement in the ratings of the SRRS life events by men and women, the old and the young, and by married and single persons were remarkably similar. There was also a high degree of correspondence in the ratings of Protestants, Catholics and Jews, and in those of Oriental and Negro minority groups with the ratings of white middle-class Americans.

31

Substantial agreement on the amount of stress associated with specific life events has also been found in research in other countries. Holmes and his colleagues translated the SRRS into French and gave the questionnaire to French-speaking inhabitants of Belgium, Switzerland and France. In addition, a Japanese translation of the SRRS was administered to a large heterogeneous sample of adults living in Hiroshima and Sandai, Japan.[15] The LCU values and ranks of the European and Japanese subjects are compared in the table on page 35 with those of the American subjects for the 15 life events ranked as most stressful by the Americans.

Environmental pollution, external and internal.

There were some differences in the ratings of life events by the American, European and Japanese subjects, but the overall ranks of the individual events by the three groups showed a significant correspondence. Indeed, the ratings of the French, Belgian and Swiss subjects in the European sample were almost identical. These cross-cultural similarities in the ratings of potentially stressful life events are especially impressive when we consider the major differences among the groups in language, family structure, religion and living conditions.

Americans, Europeans and Japanese all rated 'death of a spouse' as requiring more readjustment than any other single life event. Similarly, divorce and serving a jail term were ranked among the top four most stressful life events by all three groups. Americans and Japanese subjects generally agreed in their rankings of 14 of the 15 life events as most stressful. The Europeans agreed with the other two groups in their ratings for 12 of the 15 highest-ranked life events, and with the Americans in their ratings of 18 of the 20 highest ranked events.

Stressful life events: bitter ends...

However, interesting cultural differences were found with respect to ratings of the stress associated with retirement. Americans ranked retirement tenth in terms of the amount of readjustment that they felt would be required to cope with this event. By contrast, the French-speaking Europeans rated retirement as 17th in the severity of stress. Although the Japanese ranked retirement as 11th, the LCU value that they assigned to this event was even lower than for the Europeans.

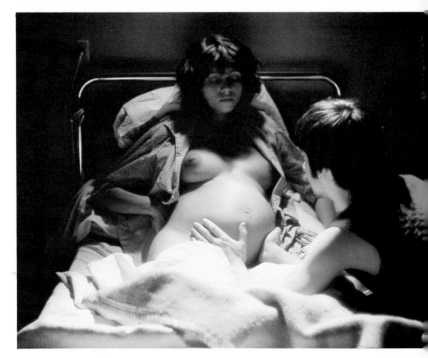

...and hard beginnings.

Why is retirement considered so stressful by Americans? Probably the answer is that Americans often feel that they have been 'shelved' when they retire; and they are concerned about becoming dependent upon their children. In contrast, many French workers look forward to retirement, secure in the knowledge that they will continue to reside with their families and to function as the heads of their households. It is also traditional in the Japanese culture to honour the head of the family; and this probably accounts for the low LCU values assigned by the Japanese to retirement and to other life events that do not disrupt or threaten family life.

A challenge or a curse?

From before birth until the last day of life stress is the inevitable accompaniment and influencer of human existence. Now that causal links between stress and illness have been established, it may be thought that this state of affairs is wholly bad and that all possible stresses ought to be obviated or mitigated in the interests of reducing the undoubted psychological and sometimes physical cost involved in adaptation to them. Such a view would not bear close examination: *some* stress, *some* anxiety is essential to the success of humanity itself.

'O dark, dark, dark, amid the blaze of noon . . .'

Like all organisms, humans must adapt and adjust if they are to survive—and it is adaptation and adjustment to stress, as challenge and as threat, that brings vitality to that survival. The sloths of the South American jungle, having few enemies and no

competition for food supply, have shown by their evolution what stress-free survival might entail—such a slowing-down of life's processes that the difference between consciousness and unconciousness is barely significant.

To hold such a view is obviously not to recommend the seeking-out of danger, deliberate involvement in stressful circumstances or the courting of anxiety: there is a level for each of them beyond which weakness and harm, rather than strengthening and vitalisation, are the results of attempts to adapt or adjust to them. In Chapter 3 the relationships between these three factors, stress, threat and anxiety, are examined in greater detail.

Ratings of stressful life events*

Life Change Unit values (with ranking)

Life Event	American	European	Japanese
Death of Spouse	100 (1)	66 (1)	108 (1)
Divorce	73 (2)	54 (3)	63 (3)
Marital Separation	65 (3)	49 (5)	46 (7)
Jail Term	63 (4)	57 (2)	72 (2)
Death of Close Family Member	63 (5)	31 (18)	57 (4)
Personal Injury or Illness	53 (6)	39 (8)	54 (5)
Marriage	50 (7)	50 (4)	50 (6)
Being Fired From Job	47 (8)	37 (9)	37 (8)
Marital Reconciliation	45 (9)	40 (7)	27 (15)
Retirement	45 (10)	31 (17)	29 (11)
Change in Health of Family Member	44 (11)	30 (20)	33 (9)
Pregnancy	40 (12)	43 (6)	27 (13)
Sexual Difficulties	39 (13)	32 (15)	31 (10)
Addition of New Family Member	39 (14)	34 (13)	18 (23)
Major Business Readjustment	39 (15)	34 (11)	28 (12)

* The complete scale of stress values measured in 'life change units' appears on pp. 116–117

3 Feeling threatened

Psychological stress is currently defined in at least two different ways. It refers first to the dangerous, potentially harmful or unpleasant external situations or conditions (stressors) that produce stress reactions, and, secondly, to the internal thoughts, judgements, emotional states and physiological processes that are evoked by stressful stimuli. Because these definitions overlap, Richard S. Lazarus, a leading authority on psychological stress, suggests that stress could be more simply described as a special kind of transaction between a person and his environment.[1] This view places equal emphasis upon the demands of the environment and the coping skills of the individual.

To understand the nature of stress, three important questions need to be clarified. First, what external conditions produce stress reactions? Second, how do stressors influence internal processes to cause stress reactions? And third, what emotional and behavioural patterns indicate the presence of stress?

In the preceding chapter, we noted that stressful circumstances are met at every stage of human growth and development. The same stressor may, of course, affect different people in different ways, but most of us agree roughly on the amount of readjustment needed to adapt to stressful life events, as was demonstrated in the table in Chapter 2 attaching a hierarchy of values (LCU) to particular stressful events. However, it is important to remember that these ratings were based on group averages. The reactions of any one person to a specific life event seem to depend very much on how he or she perceives or interprets the event: it is not only the potential danger objectively associated with the event itself which counts.

To the second question—what are the internal processes that link stressors and stress reactions?—we may answer that, although the mechanisms through which stressors assert their influence are not well understood, there is general agreement that *homeostasis* and *threat* are among the most important.

Threat and thrill are narrowly divided from one another; and a minor lapse of skill turns one to the other.

Stress and homeostasis

Homeostasis refers to the ability of an organism to maintain a relatively constant internal environment. It does this by regulating vital bodily functions like breathing and respiration, circulation of the blood, and body temperature. The vital contribution homeostasis makes to the survival of the human organism can be seen in the regulation of the fluid content of the body. The loss of 10 per cent of the body's water creates a serious medical problem, and a 20 per cent fluid loss usually results in death. Long before such dangerous levels of dehydration are reached, however, homeostatic mechanisms cause us to feel thirsty so that we drink until we have restored the optimum level of our body fluids.

Fight or flight

In the 1920s the physiologist Walter B. Cannon conducted research on the homeostatic mechanisms related to 'fight-or-flight' reactions to stressful stimuli.[2] He noted changes in the adrenal glands and in the sympathetic nervous system in both humans and animals exposed to a variety of painful ('noxious') stressors including extreme cold, lack of oxygen and emotional disturbance. He attributed these changes in internal biological processes to the activation of homeostatic mechanisms.

Cannon believed that an important function of homeostasis

Threatening behaviour has its appropriate response in fear.

was to counteract the disruptive effects caused by noxious stimulation, so that the equilibrium of the internal environment could be restored. When the homeostatic balance was upset or distorted beyond normal limits, Cannon concluded that his subjects were in a 'state of stress'. Stress, in other words, resulted from a disturbance in homeostasis.

In the mid 1930s Hans Selye began his famous experiments on the effects of stress on bodily processes. Following Cannon's earlier work, Selye conducted extensive laboratory investigations into the reactions of animals to different noxious stressors: extreme heat and cold, electric shock, surgical trauma, loss of blood, and immobilising restraint.

Each of these stressors had a specific effect on bodily reactions. But more important, Selye identified a repeated syndrome of widespread changes that were reliably induced by many *different* stressors. He concluded that these sterotyped bodily reactions to a wide variety of stressors defined a 'state of stress'.

The body's reactions to stress

The physiological changes associated with stress reactions are mediated by a nerve centre in the brain called the hypothalamus. When a stressor excites the hypothalamus, a complex chain of neural and biochemical processes is begun which alters the functioning of almost every part of the body. The autonomic nervous system, which mobilises the body for coping with stress, is directly activated by the hypothalamus, which also activates the pituitary gland. This in turn releases a biochemical agent, the

'Under the strain of competition . . .

. . . I am prone to missing my putts.'

adrenocorticotrophic hormone (ACTH), into the blood stream. Stimulated by ACTH, the adrenal gland secretes adrenalin and other biochemical agents that further arouse and mobilise the body's mechanisms.

The bodily changes which follow when this 'hypothalamus-pituitary-adrenocortical axis' is activated by a stressor prepare an animal or person for a vigorous fight-or-flight response. The heart steps up its activity, providing more blood for the brain and muscles; blood vessels close to the skin constrict and clotting time shortens, which makes severe bleeding from wounds less likely; breathing is faster and deeper, providing more oxygen; saliva and mucus dry up, increasing the size of the air passages to the lungs; and increased perspiration cools the body.

During stress reactions, many muscles tense and tighten to prepare the body for rapid and vigorous action. The pupils dilate, making the eyes more sensitive (Shakespeare gives a good description of these external changes in the Harfleur scenes in *Henry V*—'. . . Stiffen the sinews, summon up the blood, . . . lend the eye a terrible aspect . . .'). More white corpuscles are made to help fight infection. Low priority functions, like eating and the digestion of food, are suspended to conserve energy. Thus all the forces of the threatened organism are mobilised either to attack an enemy or to escape to safety.

A number of less obvious physical changes were also produced in the animals that Selye exposed to noxious stressors. They included an increase in the size of the adrenal glands, and a shrinkage of the thymus and of the lymph nodes located in the groin and armpits. Quite often, continued exposure to a strong stressor also resulted in the appearance of stomach ulcers.

Selye refers to the sum of all these bodily reactions that result from exposure to a stressor as the General Adaptation Syndrome (GAS).[3] The GAS consists of three major stages. The first is an 'alarm reaction' caused by sudden exposure to a stressful situation. Most of the changes described above occur during this initial stage.

When exposure to a stressor is prolonged, the alarm reaction is followed by a 'stage of resistance'. Signs of the alarm reaction diminish as the homeostatic mechanisms try to adjust to the stressor. But this 'resistance' uses energy which may be needed for other vital functions, so there are limits to the adaptive capacity of the organism. The resistance stage is eventually followed by the 'stage of exhaustion'. At this point, signs of the alarm reaction may reappear, but if the wear and tear of adapting to a stressor have entirely used up the coping resources of the organism, continued stress will usually result in death.

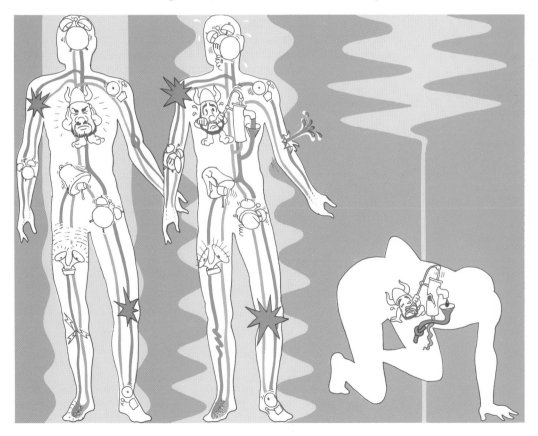

Selye's theory of the relation between stress and the GAS is widely accepted by the scientific community. But the question posed at the beginning of the chapter remains: what are the internal processes that link stressors and stress reactions? How can we explain the fact that such a diverse array of noxious stimuli caused nearly identical reactions in Selye's animals?

In a recent critique of stress research, John W. Mason has raised essentially the same question.[4] What are the mechanisms 'through which so many single "essentially different" evocative agents could transmit the common "message of stress"?' In Mason's view, it is *emotional arousal* that transmits the 'message of stress' which activates the GAS.

What kind of emotional reactions come between stressors and stress reactions, and how are these particular emotions aroused? We have previously seen that a state of anxiety is evoked when a stressor is seen as a threat: the appraisal of a situation as threatening appears to be the critical factor that intervenes between stressors and stress reactions, and results in the arousal of an anxiety state and the activation of Selye's GAS.

Stress and threat

A friend for one but a foe for another

Reactions to stress depend on whether or not a particular situation is seen as threatening. The concept of threat refers to a person's *subjective* appraisal of an event as potentially harmful.[5]

Of course, threat appraisals are influenced by the objective facts of a situation; and stressors that are *objectively* dangerous are generally also perceived as threatening by most people. But the thoughts and memories that are stimulated by the situation and the individual's coping skills and previous experience with similar circumstances can have an even greater impact.

'Which way is east?'—disorientation can rapidly produce high levels of anxiety.

If an objectively dangerous situation is to be appraised as threatening, the potential danger must be noticed. A pedestrian crossing a busy street who suddenly sees a speeding car approaching will undoubtedly judge the situation to be extremely threatening, and take evasive action. But, if the pedestrian fails to notice the speeding car, the unnoticed danger will not be subjectively appraised as threatening, and a serious accident may well be the result.

The context in which a potential danger is encountered will also influence the extent to which a situation is thought to be threatening. The same stimulus may be seen as a threat by one person, a challenge by another, and as largely irrelevant by a third. For example, an unarmed man unexpectedly confronted by a lion in the jungle is likely to see this situation as extremely dangerous, and to react to it with intense fear and anxiety. But the same lion may induce a sense of challenge and exhilaration in

For him, an intense challenge; but simply entertainment to the spectators.

a big game hunter; and mere amusement in children at the zoo.

The experience of threat, then, is essentially a state of mind. It has two main characteristics: it is future oriented (that is, it generally involves the anticipation of a potentially harmful event that has not yet happened); and it consists of mental processes, which include perception, thought, memory and judgement.

Perception and appraisal of threat

In order to understand how mental processes contribute to the subjective appraisal of a particular situation, let us consider a simple example. The interpretation of the drawing presented in the figure on this page will depend on what is perceived as the *figure* and what is seen as the *background*. If one glances at the drawing as a whole, it may well be seen as a flower vase or goblet. However, a good look at the sides of the 'vase' will reveal the profiles of two people.

While you are looking at the 'vase', notice that the white space in the centre of the figure appears closer and, in a vague way, more solid than when you look at the 'faces'. Focusing on the two profiles seems to make the central space recede and the faces stand out. Depending on whether you focus upon the white area or the dark profiles, there is an important difference in what is perceived. Yet nothing in the drawing itself or in the structure of our brain or nervous system can account for the involuntary alternation—the 'flip-flop'—between the two distinctly different perceptions. Our interpretation of the drawing depends upon the particular features on which we focus our attention, and on previous learning and memory that provide us with the concepts of a vase or goblet and a human profile.

While some of what we see is determined by the object itself, our needs can also influence perception. For example, a hungry person is more likely to notice food than is someone who has just finished a heavy meal; and the mirage of a lake or an oasis is common to thirsty travellers. Physiological needs make us more attentive to those aspects of the environment that will satisfy these needs.

Personality characteristics and emotions can also play an important role in how we interpret a particular situation. For example, a distrustful, suspicious person might see the profiles in the 'figure-ground phenomenon' as two people engaged in malicious gossip or concocting a sinister plot: what is essentially a neutral stimulus may be interpreted as a source of potential danger or harm. The process of attributing one's own personality characteristics to other people or things is called *projection*: it provides the underlying basis for the use of tests in personality assessment such as the Rorschach ink blots.

When the cues associated with a situation are seen as signs of impending danger, the situation will be experienced as threatening. Threat reactions serve an important function when they are based on a realistic appraisal of present or future danger: they then produce emotional arousal that mobilises an individual to take actions to avoid harm. But even when there is no objective danger, the appraisal of a situation as threatening will transmit the message of stress. It will sound the alarm that leads to the arousal of anxiety and to the activation of the GAS.

The 'Spirit of Ecstasy', trademark of success . . .

. . . and the trademark of failure, just plain (methylated) spirit.

Threat and anxiety

Of the questions raised at the beginning of this chapter, only the third remains to be considered: what emotional and behavioural patterns indicate the presence of stress?

Whenever an event or situation is seen as threatening, irrespective of whether the danger is real or imagined, the sense of threat will lead to an unpleasant emotional reaction—the arousal of an anxiety state. Anxiety states are easy to recognise in oneself or (by report) in others because they comprise a unique combination of unpleasant feelings and thoughts, as well as the physiological processes we described above. The sufferer feels apprehensive, tense, upset, frightened and nervous, and tends—naturally—to worry about the specific circumstances that aroused the anxiety state.[6] In addition to thoughts about the physical or psychological damage that might result from the real or imagined danger, relatively unimportant matters may also come to mind, stimulated indirectly by the general level of emotional arousal.

Anxiety states vary in intensity and fluctuate over time.[7] Calmness and serenity indicate an *absence* of anxiety. Tension, apprehension and nervousness accompany moderate levels of anxiety. Intense feelings of fear and fright and associated panic behaviour characterise very high levels of anxiety. The intensity and duration of an anxiety state will depend on the stressors that impinge on a person and on that person's interpretation of those stressors as personally dangerous or threatening.[8]

Behaviour resulting from anxiety states includes restlessness, trembling, shortness of breath, fearful facial expression, muscular tension (tics and twitches), lack of energy and fatigue. The physiological changes that underlie these behavioural manifestations are essentially the same as those that occur when the 'hypothalamus-pituitary-adrenocortical axis' is activated in stress reactions. Heart rate increases, blood pressure rises, breathing is faster and deeper, muscles tense and tighten, and the pupils dilate.

The similarity of the physiological changes in anxiety states and in stress reactions supports Mason's observation that emotional arousal transmits the message of stress. The fact that threat and anxiety intervene between stressors and stress reactions conforms with Lazarus' definition of stress as a special kind of transaction between person and environment. This transaction begins with the interpretation of a situation as threatening, and results in the arousal of an anxiety state with its associated physiological changes. Because anxiety states are experienced as unpleasant, they prompt people to behave in a way that will help them to avoid or minimise the threat.

Even when situations are objectively benign, they can evoke intense levels of anxiety in people who for some reason see them as potentially dangerous. For example, a telephone call in the middle of the night might be highly threatening for a woman whose husband is in hospital suffering from a serious illness. When the phone is answered and it is discovered that the caller has dialled a wrong number, there will be a sigh of relief, signifying the reduction of anxiety. However, the recipient of the call may have difficulty in going back to sleep because of anxious thoughts about her husband's illness and the tragic consequences for the entire family if he died.

Answers

To the three questions about stress and anxiety posed in this chapter tentative answers can now be given. First, it is not possible to specify the external conditions that determine when a stress reaction will be produced, because stress reactions depend on an interpretation of conditions as threatening, whatever the objective characteristics of the situation may be.

Second, the internal processes that link stressors to stress reactions appear to be threat, disturbances in homeostasis, and anxiety.

Third, the emotional and behavioural patterns that indicate the presence of stress are: subjective feelings of tension, apprehension and fear, worry reactions, and physiological and behavioural changes that we associate with anxiety. Stress, therefore, can be defined by transactions between the person and the environment in which stressors are linked to anxiety reactions by the perception of threat.

Drawn faces living with fear, and pain, and defeat: prisoners of war in Vietnam.

4   Fear and anxiety

The 20th century has been called the 'age of anxiety'. In fact, concern with fear and anxiety is as old as humanity itself. The concept of fear was clearly represented in ancient Egyptian hieroglyphics, and there are frequent references to fear in the Bible and in the writings of early Greek and Roman philosophers.[1]

Perhaps the earliest recorded recognition of the importance of anxiety as a determinant of behaviour is in an 11th-century treatise of the Arab philosopher Ala Ibn Hazm of Cordova, in which he proposes the universality of anxiety as a basic condition of human existence and a prime motivator of what we do.

> I have constantly tried to single out one end in human actions which all men unanimously hold as good and which they all seek. I have found only this: The aim of escaping anxiety ... Not only have I discovered that all humanity considers this good and desirable, but also ... no one is moved to act or moved to speak a single word who does not hope by means of this action or word to release anxiety from his spirit.[2]

But while fear and anxiety have long been regarded as important reactions to stress, there is still a great deal of confusion and controversy about the definitions of these terms. In this chapter an attempt will be made to clarify similarities and differences in these concepts. Individual differences in anxiety proneness will be examined, as well as the important distinction between anxiety as an emotional state and anxiety as a personality trait.

Fear and human evolution

Charles Darwin regarded fear as a fundamental human emotion. In his classic book *The Expression of Emotions in Man and Animals*, published in 1872, Darwin reasoned that the potential for experiencing fear was an inherent characteristic of both humans and animals.[3] Within the framework of his theory of evolution, the function of fear was to arouse and mobilise the organism for coping with external danger.

Darwin believed that the essential characteristics of fear reactions had evolved over countless generations through a process of natural selection. He described a number of typical

49

manifestations of fear including rapid heart palpitation, dilation of the pupils, erection of the hair, mouth dryness, increased perspiration, peculiar facial expression, and changes in voice quality. Darwin also noted that fear reactions vary in intensity—from attention and mild apprehension or surprise to what he described as an extreme 'agony of terror'.

Many of the characteristics of fear that were described by Darwin are also found in Cannon's 'fight-or-flight response', and in the alarm reaction that initiates Selye's General Adaptation Syndrome. However, whereas Darwin placed greater emphasis on observable physical manifestations of fear, Cannon and Selye, who worked mainly with laboratory animals, were concerned primarily with the physiological and biochemical changes that occurred within the body.

The adaptive function of a fear reaction is to provide a signal that warns the organism that something must be done—either to escape or to eliminate a potential danger. Thus, when a caveman encountered a sabre-toothed tiger, the fear reaction sounded an internal alarm, warning him that immediate action was required to avoid the danger, or to attack and destroy its source. But it has to be, within quite narrow limits, the right amount of fear: too little or too much can have serious consequences. Too little might have led the caveman to a foolhardy attack on the tiger. Too much might throw him into a panic or, even worse, into that frozen immobility that would make him an easy prey. In these circumstances, even if he managed to escape, his intense fear might persist and force him to remain in his cave, either to starve to death or at least preclude the hunt for a suitable mate with whom to propagate his species.

According to the theory of evolution and natural selection, organisms that either under-react or over-react to dangerous situations are more likely to perish and thus be 'selected out' of the group. Conversely, the caveman who experienced an appropriate degree of fear that facilitated his adjustment to an objective danger would be more likely to survive. Only survivors can pass on their adaptive qualities to future generations.

Fear and objective anxiety

Fear has been the subject of investigation and interest since ancient times. But *anxiety* was not fully recognised as a distinct and pervasive condition of humanity until the present century.[4] Obviously the fact of anxiety has been around since the first evolution of the species *homo*, just as the fact of cancer has; but just as cancer was, until investigative medicine became sufficiently sophisticated to identify it, often subsumed in such general descriptions as 'galloping consumption' or 'bloody flux' or 'running sore', so anxiety was seen as merely an aspect of fear.

As with so much else that we now take for granted, psychology was a child of two 19th century phenomena—the rapid growth of the spirit of sceptical intellectual inquiry and the social conditions accompanying the industrialisation of western

'I have this nightmare, you see; then, in the morning . . .'

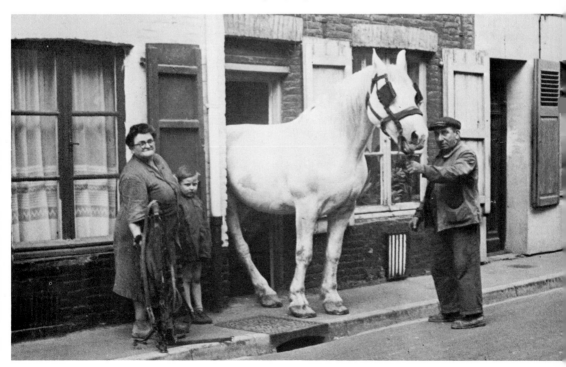

51

All smiles—but in some of them it is the rictus of extreme terror.

Europe. Rapid technological change, rapid urbanisation and rapid turnover of ideas about man's place in the world all contributed to the unfixing of the points by which, in previous centuries, a largely rural population with unchanging ways had taken its mental bearings. Such 'alienation' is a fruitful breeding ground of anxiety, as of other conditions we now call 'psychological problems'. When the first systematic psychologists began their work, therefore, there was plenty of material for their investigations—sufficient for the most famous of them, Sigmund Freud, to be able to make a distinction between two afflicting conditions, fear and anxiety.

For it was Freud who first proposed a critical role for anxiety in the formation of neurotic and psychosomatic conditions.[5] For him, anxiety was the 'fundamental phenomenon and the central problem of neurosis'.[6] He came to consider that understanding anxiety was 'the most difficult task that has been set us', a task whose solution required the 'introduction of the right abstract ideas, and of their application to the raw material of observation so as to bring order and lucidity into it'.[7] The complexity of this task, and Freud's personal commitment to it, were reflected in the fact that his theoretical views on the subject evolved over a period of nearly 50 years, were continually modified, and were never considered by him as complete.

Freud regarded anxiety as 'something felt'—a specific unpleasant emotional state or condition of the human organism. Anxiety states were broadly defined as 'all that is covered by the word "nervousness"', and they included experiential, physiological and behavioural components.[8]

The experiential qualities associated with an anxiety state

consisted of subjective feelings of tension, apprehension and worry. The physiological arousal and behavioural manifestations that contributed to the unpleasantness of anxiety states included heart palpitations (tachycardia), disturbances of respiration, sweating, restlessness, tremor and shuddering, nausea and vertigo (dizziness). Many of the physiological and behavioural symptoms that Freud attributed to anxiety states were, indeed, quite similar to the characteristics of fear that had been described by Darwin.

Anxiety states can be distinguished from other unpleasant emotions such as anger, sorrow or grief by their unique combination of experiential, physiological, and behavioural manifestations. While Freud considered the physiological and behavioural symptoms to be essential *components* of anxiety states, it was the subjective, experiential qualities—the *feelings* of apprehension, tension and dread—that gave anxiety reactions a special 'character of unpleasure'. Using the probing introspective methods of psychoanalysis, Freud tried to discover in the childhood experiences of his patients 'the historical element' which connected anxiety reactions with the stressors that caused or reactivated them.[9]

Indistinguishable states from the external signs; but quite different on the inside: Beatle fan at a concert (left) and sole survivor of a family tragedy (right).

In his early formulations, Freud theorised that anxiety resulted from the discharge of repressed sexual energy which he called *libido*. When sexual energy produced mental images (lustful ideas) that were seen as threatening, these ideas were put out of mind or *repressed*. Blocked from normal expression, libidinal energy accumulated and was automatically transformed into 'free-floating' anxiety, or into symptoms—sometimes physical—that were anxiety equivalents.

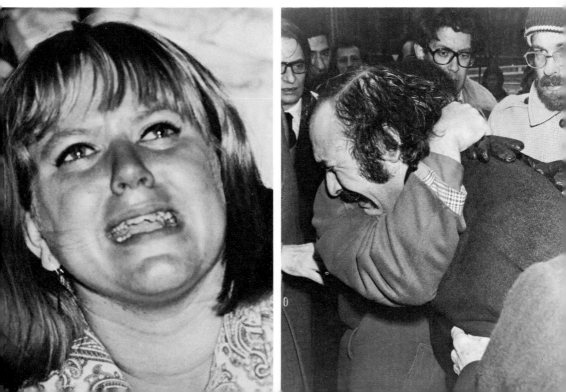

Freud subsequently modified his views to emphasise the critical role of anxiety as a response to the presence of danger. The perceived presence of danger—either from the external environment or from internal feelings or thoughts—evoked an anxiety state; and this unpleasant emotional reaction served to warn the individual that some form of adjustment was necessary. Thus, like Darwin, Freud emphasised the usefulness of fear and anxiety in helping a person to adapt to danger.

In his later conception of anxiety, Freud called attention to two potential sources of danger—the external world and a person's own internal impulses. If the source of danger was in the external world, this resulted in an *objective* anxiety reaction. Anxiety reactions that were evoked by forbidden or unacceptable internal impulses were called *neurotic* anxiety.

For Freud, objective anxiety and fear were synonymous; both terms referred to the unpleasant emotional state that was aroused when injury or harm from some external danger was anticipated. Whenever a real danger in the external world was consciously perceived as threatening, this resulted in an objective anxiety reaction. Thus:

$$\textbf{External danger} \rightarrow \textbf{Perception of danger} \rightarrow \textbf{Objective anxiety}$$

According to Freud, an important characteristic of an objective anxiety (or fear) reaction is that the intensity of the unpleasant emotional state is proportional to the magnitude of the external danger that causes it. In other words, the greater the external danger, the more intense the resulting objective anxiety can be expected to be.

Neurotic anxiety

If objective anxiety is a reaction or response to a real danger in the external world, what is neurotic anxiety? According to Freud, punishment for the expression of normal sexual and aggressive impulses, especially during early childhood, may result in objective anxiety being converted into neurotic anxiety. In neurotic anxiety, the source of the danger is internal rather than external, and the person is not consciously aware of the stressor.

Let us consider an example of how objective anxiety is converted into neurotic anxiety. A three-year-old boy has enjoyed the exclusive attention of his parents but must now share their affection with a new addition to the family. When his demands for attention are temporarily ignored by his mother, who is busy attending to the needs of the baby, he picks up one of the building blocks with which he is playing and throws it in the direction of the baby's crib. This both frightens and angers his mother, who vigorously slaps his hand and severely scolds him.

'No, I'm not neurotic, just terribly hurt.'

55

The transaction between the boy and his environment can be analysed as follows. First, when the child sees that his mother is spending most of her time with the new baby, he feels neglected and angry (*angry impulse*). Acting on his angry feelings, the child throws the block in the direction of the source of his frustration (*aggressive behaviour*). Since he is immediately punished for this misdeed, he accurately sees his mother as a source of *external danger*. On later occasions, *whenever* the child has angry feelings or thoughts that would result in aggressive behaviour for which he might be punished by his mother, he will experience fear about being punished, that is, *objective anxiety*. This sequence of events may be diagrammed as follows:

$$\textbf{Angry} \rightarrow \textbf{Aggressive} \rightarrow \textbf{External} \rightarrow \textbf{Objective}$$
$$\textbf{impulse} \qquad \textbf{behaviour} \qquad \textbf{danger} \qquad \textbf{anxiety}$$

Objective anxiety is useful if it helps a child to avoid punishment by inhibiting the expression of inappropriate impulses. Learning to inhibit the tendency to attack or strike out against sources of frustration is an essential part of the socialisation of every child. But severe punishment of aggressive acts can result in intense neurotic anxiety reactions that inhibit normal and often desirable assertive behaviour even when there is little or no real danger.

Neurotic anxiety reactions are originally based on objective anxiety. The process of converting objective anxiety into neurotic anxiety begins when *internal* stimuli or *cues* associated with previously punished behaviours arouse *objective anxiety*. Since objective anxiety reactions are experienced as unpleasant, these reactions initiate mental and behavioural activities that are designed to reduce or alleviate the unpleasantness. If efforts to reduce objective anxiety result in the *repression of internal cues*, that is, banishing from awareness all thoughts or memories associated with the previously punished behaviours, the stage is set for the later appearance of neurotic anxiety. The reason for this is that repression is never final or complete, and a partial breakdown in repression permits fragments or symbolic representations of repressed traumatic events to erupt into awareness. These *derivatives of repressed thoughts* are the danger signals that evoke *neurotic anxiety* reactions. Thus, the process of converting objective anxiety into neurotic anxiety involves the following sequence of events:

Internal cues → **Objective anxiety** → **Repression of internal cues**

Breakdown in repression → **Derivatives of repressed thoughts** → **Neurotic anxiety**

Since the actual memory of the repressed traumatic event remains buried in the unconscious, the source of danger in neurotic anxiety is not recognised. Consequently, neurotic anxiety reactions are typically experienced as 'objectless' or without cause.

Let us now return to the three-year-old boy in our previous example. Suppose on some future occasion that the child feels angry in the presence of one of his teachers and these feelings precipitate an anxiety state even though there is no real danger of being punished by the teacher. This neurotic anxiety reaction happens because a breakdown in repression has resulted in derivatives of the child's repressed memories of punishment becoming conscious in the presence of his teacher. However, since the memory of being punished for expressing anger in the presence of his mother remains repressed, he will be unaware that the true source of danger which evoked the neurotic anxiety reaction resides in his own angry impulses, rather than the objective situation.

An important difference between neurotic and objective anxiety is that the intensity of the emotional state associated with neurotic anxiety is always greater than would be warranted by the real or objective danger that evokes the reaction. Since the intensity of the emotional reaction in fear or objective anxiety is proportional to the actual danger, whenever a person reacts with a high level of anxiety to a situation that is only mildly stressful, the source of the danger must be associated with repressed internal feelings rather than with an external stressor.

Phobias

Phobias are examples of neurotic anxiety reactions in which an intense state of fear is produced by a specific object or situation that is in fact relatively harmless. When exposed to the feared object or situation, a phobic person experiences an anxiety attack that leads him to take elaborate steps to avoid the phobic object. Since intense anxiety is aroused by a stimulus that is relatively harmless, phobic reactions are clearly 'irrational' or pathological.

There are many different types of phobias. Claustrophobia, for example, is an irrational fear of enclosed places such as small rooms or closets, elevators, or even vehicles such as automobiles or aeroplanes. Other common phobias are acrophobia (fear of heights), agoraphobia (fear of open spaces), numerous animal phobias such as fear of cats, dogs, snakes, spiders and other creatures, and even phobias about inanimate objects (dead leaves, paper, etc.).

Suppose a small child is locked in a closet by a playmate and not discovered by his parents until hours later. This experience is extremely frightening and arouses an intense state of anxiety. After being released from the closet, the child continues to have

A fine breeding ground for phobias and panic fear.

terrifying memories about the traumatic experience. In time, the child learns to reduce the anxiety that is aroused when he thinks about being locked in the closet by repressing from consciousness any memory of the frightening experience. However, as previously explained, repression is not complete or final, and cues associated with small enclosed places subsequently trigger neurotic anxiety reactions that are similar to the objective anxiety that the child experienced when he was trapped in the closet. This is claustrophobia.

Phobias tend to endure because they cause the phobic person to avoid the feared object or situation. Prevented from discovering that the frightening situations which evoke these neurotic anxiety reactions are in fact harmless, the phobic person continues to feel anxious whenever cues associated with the original traumatic experience are encountered. Moreover, every time the phobic object is successfully avoided anxiety is reduced and the phobic individual's determination to avoid the feared situation increased.

Neurotic or real?

The intensity of the anxiety state in phobic reactions is obviously much greater than would be expected on the basis of the real danger. But it is often difficult to determine whether or not an anxiety reaction is neurotic or in fact proportional to the objective danger. To do so would require careful assessment of the amount of real danger associated with a particular stressor and precise measurement of the intensity of the resulting anxiety reaction.

Consider, for example, how difficult it would be to classify as neurotic or objective an intense anxiety reaction that was suddenly evident in a woman who had been relaxing at the beach listening to the radio, from which comes news of an aircraft crash in Africa. At first glance, the woman's behaviour might appear to be extremely neurotic. However, when we learn that her husband is at the time a passenger on an aircraft flying to an African destination, her anxiety reaction now seems much more proportional to the objective psychological danger. (It will be recalled that the death of a spouse was consistently rated as more stressful than any other single life event by Americans, Europeans and Japanese.)[10]

In both objective and neurotic anxiety, the intensity of the unpleasant emotional state is proportional to the *subjective* appraisal of the amount of danger associated with the stimulus that evokes these reactions. The interpretation of a situation as more or less threatening will depend upon its objective characteristics, the thoughts and memories that are stimulated by the situation, the individual's coping skills and previous experience with similar circumstances.

It is important to understand that neurotic and objective anxiety differ in terms of the internal and external stressors that evoke them, the complexity of the processes that intervene between the stressors and the anxiety states that are aroused, and whether or not the reaction is proportional to the real danger. However, the unpleasant emotional states that are experienced in both kinds of reaction are so similar as to be practically indistinguishable.

Individual differences in anxiety proneness

State anxiety, as previously noted, refers to unpleasant emotional reactions to specific stress. While everyone experiences state anxiety from time to time, there are substantial differences among people in the frequency and the intensity with which these states are experienced. The term *trait anxiety* has been used to describe individual differences in anxiety proneness, that is, in the tendency to see the world as dangerous and in the frequency that state anxiety is experienced over a long period of time.[11]

Fairground thrills—fun for some . . .

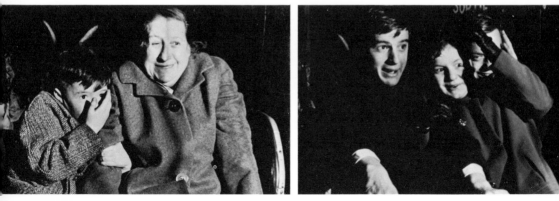

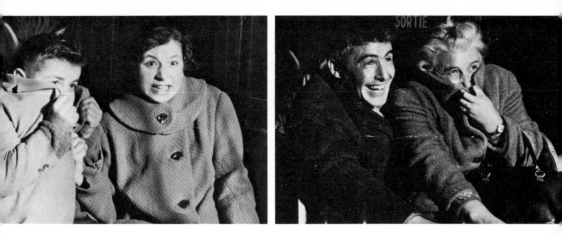

... but for others only pleasurable when they stop.

To clarify the distinction between anxiety as a personality trait and as a transitory emotional state, consider the statement 'Mr. Smith is anxious'. This statement may be interpreted as meaning either that Smith is anxious *now* or that Smith is an anxious person. If Smith is 'anxious now', at this very moment, this implies that he is experiencing an unpleasant emotional state. But if Smith is 'an anxious person', his average level of state anxiety would generally be higher than that of most other people; and unless he lives in a very sheltered environment, Smith is likely to experience anxiety states more often than others. However, even though Smith may be an *anxious person*, he may or may not be *anxious now*: this will depend on whether he interprets his *present* circumstances as dangerous.

Persons high in trait anxiety ('A-Trait') tend to view the world as more dangerous than people with low trait anxiety; and they respond to their perceptions of threat with more frequent increases in state anxiety ('A-State'). Since high A-Trait people tend to see many different situations as threatening, they are especially vulnerable to stress. High A-Trait individuals are also more likely to experience neurotic anxiety in which derivatives of repressed thoughts or memories of dangerous situations precipitate additional A-State reactions.

Individuals with very high trait anxiety—such as psychoneurotics or people suffering from depression—are high in state anxiety almost all of the time. However, even they have defences against anxiety that occasionally leave them relatively free of it. For example, when anxious persons are occupied with a nonthreatening task, like a noncompetitive but absorbing game, they may be diverted for a time from the internal stimuli that otherwise constantly cue state anxiety responses. Thus, when high A-Trait persons do not feel threatened, they will not experience elevations in state anxiety.

In the following chapter, we examine the complex relationship between trait and state anxiety, and the psychological mechanisms that people customarily use in adjusting or adapting to intense anxiety states.

5 Patterns of adjustment

So far we have defined significant pieces in the puzzle of stress and anxiety. In general terms, stress and anxiety refer to complex transactions between people and their environments. They involve: potentially harmful external dangers or pressures (stressors); internal thoughts, memories, and physiological processes; and the intense unpleasant emotional reactions evoked by stressful stimuli.

We have seen that stressful environmental circumstances must be faced every day and at every stage of human development. While the amount of stress attributed to specific life events—such as divorce or the death of a spouse—is remarkably similar among people from different cultures, there are also substantial differences in how people react to stress.

The potential for experiencing anxiety reactions has emerged over countless generations during the course of human evolution. Whenever a stimulus or situation is seen as threatening, this arouses a state of anxiety—an unpleasant emotional state which consists of feelings of tension, apprehension, nervousness and worry, accompanied by widespread physiological changes.

Objective anxiety reactions are proportional in intensity to an external danger; these reactions are *adaptive* because they serve as danger signals that mobilise a person for coping with harmful situations. Neurotic anxiety reactions, such as 'irrational fears' and phobias, occur when the source of danger stems primarily from thoughts or memories of repressed traumatic experiences, rather than from an external stressor. The intensity of the anxiety state in neurotic anxiety is proportional to the perceived internal threat; but it is substantially greater than would be warranted by the objective external danger. Thus, neurotic anxiety reactions are *maladaptive* because they mobilise the individual to adjust to repressed memories of dangers that no longer exist.

How we cope with anxiety

In this chapter, we look more closely at the relationship between anxiety and adjustment, and consider the psychological mechanisms that people use to avoid, alleviate, or defend against anxiety states. Rating scales that have been developed to measure 'state' and 'trait' anxiety are provided which can be used to measure

'I, a stranger and afraid
In a world I never made.'

your own level of state and trait anxiety, together with tables, by means of which you can compare your anxiety scores with those of other people.

Stressors, the state–trait concept and adjustment

The diagram on pages 78 and 79 provides a framework for examining the complex relationship between stressors, state and trait anxiety, and adjustment.[1] Each of the boxes in the diagram represents a critical element in stress transactions that link stressful stimuli with the internal processes and behavioural reactions that they evoke. The arrows in the diagram refer to the sequence of interactions among the components, and to possible influences of one element upon another.

The arousal of an anxiety state (A-State) involves a complex sequence of internal events. This process may be initiated by either *external* or *internal stimuli*. Examples of external stressors might be the prospect of imminent injury or death faced by a soldier in battle or the strong verbal rebuke administered to a worker making a mistake.

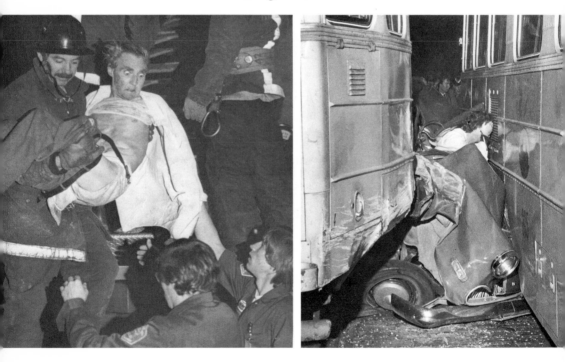

The agony of fear, seen (left), and (right) barely imaginable.

An internal stimulus that causes an individual to anticipate a harmful situation may also evoke a high level of state anxiety. For example, a student who suddenly realises that he has forgotten to prepare for an examination to be given in the next class period would undoubtedly experience a large increase in A-State. Nightmares can also evoke intense A-State reactions which usually abate when the dreamer awakes.

Any external or internal stimulus that is *cognitively appraised* as threatening will evoke an A-State reaction. The intensity and duration of this emotional reaction will be proportional to the amount of threat that the situation poses for the individual and the persistence of the evoking stimuli. The objective characteristics of a situation, the thoughts and memories that are elicited or recalled, and the individual's coping skills and previous experiences in dealing with similar circumstances all contribute to the appraisal of a situation as more or less threatening.

Horror as a man dies: 'Never send to know for whom the bell tolls; it tolls for thee.'

Individual differences in anxiety proneness, that is, trait anxiety (A-Trait), also contribute to threat appraisals. While situations that involve physical dangers are interpreted as threatening by most people, circumstances in which personal adequacy is evaluated are more likely to be perceived as threatening by people who are high in A-Trait than by low A-Trait persons.[2] In general, people who are high in trait anxiety are more vulnerable to being evaluated by others because they are low in self-esteem and lack confidence in themselves.

In the examples described in an earlier chapter, high A-Trait contributed to the anxiety states that were experienced by the young woman taking an examination and by the young man applying for a position as a motor mechanic. While important tests and job interviews are seen as moderately stressful by most people, the intense anxiety reactions experienced by these two were much greater than the real danger warranted. Such irrational or neurotic anxiety reactions are often experienced by people who are high in trait anxiety in situations in which there is a risk of failure or which involve being evaluated by others.

What are the origins of individual differences in trait anxiety? Childhood experiences and early parent–child relationships related to withdrawal of love and negative evaluations by teachers and peers seem to be especially important.[3] Thus, beginning in elementary school, the young examinee as a child felt rejected when her mother withdrew her love at times that the girl's school work was not up to the high standards set by her parents. Although the young car mechanic was accepted by his family, he was criticised by his teachers and constantly ridiculed by his classmates because he spoke English badly.

Anxiety and adjustment

High levels of state anxiety, being extremely unpleasant, serve to initiate behaviour designed to eliminate or reduce the anxiety. An obvious way of reducing an anxiety state aroused by an external danger is to modify the environment so that the danger is eliminated. Thus, when a startled hunter kills a rattlesnake that has invaded his campsite, he will surely experience a substantial reduction in A-State.

Another way of reducing an anxiety state that is evoked by an external stressor is to avoid the source of danger. A young boy who is frequently beaten up by a neighbourhood bully on his way home from school will probably decide to take an alternative route that enables him to avoid the threat of further beatings. Though he must invest more time and energy in returning home each day, the price is worth paying to reduce his anxiety level and the real danger posed by the bully.

You can run away from what you fear—or summon up the blood˚ and meet it head-on.

In these two examples, the level of A-State was reduced through overt *behaviour* that altered the individual's relationship with his environment. In killing the rattlesnake or taking the long way home, a source of real danger in the external world was eliminated or avoided. But people also adjust to stressful situations by engaging in unconscious psychological manoeuvres designed to alter the way they see a situation so that it will seem less threatening. Such processes, which modify the way a threatening

'A crowd flowed over London Bridge, so many,
I had not thought death had undone so many.'
(Eliot: The Waste Land)

situation is seen without in fact dealing with the actual source of danger, are called *defence mechanisms*.[4] To the extent that a defence mechanism is successful, the circumstances that evoke anxiety will be seen as less threatening, and there will be a corresponding reduction in A-State intensity. But the individual must pay the price of wasting energy by investing it in internal psychological processes that are devoted entirely to reducing state anxiety. Since the underlying problems that caused the anxiety remain unchanged, psychological defence mechanisms are almost always inefficient and often maladaptive.

In general, psychological defence mechanisms modify, distort, or render unconscious the feelings, thoughts and memories that would otherwise provoke anxiety. *Repression* is the most basic defence against internal psychological threats: it is the primary means of banishing anxiety-arousing stimuli from the conscious mind. But there are other defence mechanisms (some of which involve repression) which also seek to prevent disturbing materials from entering consciousness.

Repression and denial

In an earlier chapter, we described the psychological events surrounding the actions of a three-year-old boy. He became angry because he was neglected by his mother, and threw a building block at his sibling's crib. As a consequence of this aggressive behaviour, he was scolded and slapped by his mother. On future occasions—whenever feelings, thoughts, or memories associated with the punishment were recalled—the boy felt intensely anxious. To protect himself against these unpleasant anxiety states, the events that were originally associated with punishment were expelled from his consciousness. Once repressed, these events were no longer able to trigger (cue) an anxiety state. So long as repression is successful in keeping the threatening cues out of awareness, it will protect the boy from anxiety arousal by this source of danger.

Repression is the process by which feelings, thoughts, or memories that arouse intense states of anxiety are banished from consciousness. A dental appointment may be forgotten, or the name of the teacher of a course that was failed may be unrecallable, because repression prevents memories of such unpleasant experiences from being registered in the conscious mind. If a person is no longer aware of the cues associated with a painful or traumatic past experience, repression can be effective in defending against anxiety.

A person who uses repression is, in effect, keeping certain

Rock concerts often provide the grounds for getting your repressions out into the open.

Invulnerable in armour ...

threatening internal stimuli locked up in the unconscious mind. His main concern is controlling his own anxiety, rather than coping with the actual source of danger. When repression is effective, the individual will be unaware of the repressed feelings, thoughts, and memories, and so will not experience anxiety from these sources. However, if repression is weak, or there is a partial breakdown in repression, derivatives of the original experience can once again precipitate an anxiety state.

The defence mechanism of *denial* is similar to repression in that it defends against anxiety by putting threatening stimuli into the unconscious. But denial is a more primitive defence than repression in that it causes the individual to distort external reality as well, blocking a disturbing stressor out of awareness by failing to recognise that a real threat exists. For example, a worker who is severely and repeatedly reprimanded for performing poorly on the job literally fails to hear his supervisor's criticism. By denying the existence of the criticism, the worker protects himself from the thought of losing his job, which would arouse unbearable anxiety.

Examples of extreme denial have been observed in soldiers in combat who fail to recognise the real danger of being injured or killed and seem to be convinced that they are invulnerable to harm. In the Vietnam conflict, psychiatrist Peter Bourne described a Green Beret who developed the belief that he had divine protection from harm.[5] The strength of the man's denial was reflected in his riding a bicycle 20 miles a day over enemy-controlled jungle roads to receive communion from a Vietnamese priest.

Rationalisation and intellectualisation

... and as frail as the thickness of skin.

The mechanism of *rationalisation* is a form of psychological defence in which a person gives logically acceptable but false

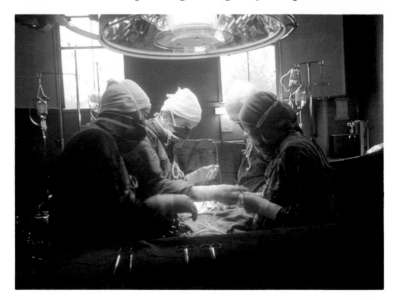

reasons for his or her actions, because facing up to the true reasons would arouse a high level of state anxiety. For example, a discharged employee might rationalise that he 'quit' his job because of a 'personality conflict' between himself and his supervisor. To admit that he lacked the skills and competence that were needed to perform the work would precipitate too much anxiety.

'Sour grapes' is the name given to a frequently encountered form of rationalisation. In the familiar Aesop fable, the fox who was unable to reach the grapes rationalised that they were sour; so was less frustrated and disappointed by his failure. Such rationalisations may be expressed in private to oneself, spoken aloud to other people, or manifested directly in behaviour.

The use of 'sour grapes' rationalisation to avoid anxiety may be illustrated by the young man whose fiancée breaks their engagement. In working through his intense state of anxiety—based partly on feelings of inadequacy from being rejected—the young man 'reasons' that the girl who refused him had innumerable faults and would undoubtedly have made a poor wife. Through the process of rationalisation he convinces himself that he never really wanted to marry the girl and that it was he who broke off the relationship. With this interpretation of the broken engagement the young man no longer feels inadequate or anxious over being rejected.

The mechanism of *intellectualisation*—which is closely related to rationalisation—involves the use of a highly abstract reasoning process to reduce anxiety. For example, a college student participating in a psychology experiment was told that he would receive a strong electric shock while he worked on a memory task.[6] In an interview conducted after the experiment, the student explained that he was at first very disturbed when he was told that he would be shocked. However, after thinking about the circumstances of the experiment he 'reasoned' (intellectualised) that it was unlikely that he would actually be shocked, and that even if he were shocked it would not be very painful 'because university officials would not permit this'.

The student's initial appraisal of the situation as extremely threatening resulted in an immediate acceleration in his heart rate, which was monitored in the experiment in order to measure changes in state anxiety. Subsequent to his intellectualised reappraisal, there was a substantial drop in his heart rate, indicating a corresponding reduction in his level of A-State.

Reaction formation

*More rationalisation . . .
Putting a brave
face on things.*

Reaction formation is a complicated defence mechanism: a person represses unacceptable impulses or feeling and then expresses, usually in an exaggerated form, feelings that are incompatible with or opposite to those that were repressed. In expressing feelings that are the opposite of the repressed impulses—for example, replacing intense hate by ostentatious love—this mechanism protects the individual from becoming aware of the unacceptable feelings.

Extreme forms of behaviour of any kind may reflect reaction formations. For example, an overprotective mother, apparently obsessed with the welfare and safety of her child, may actually harbour intense feelings of anger and hostility towards the child, which are repressed because they arouse intolerable anxiety and guilt. Similarly, a man who feels inadequate and insecure in his relationships with other people may develop a 'tough guy' façade—adopting a manner that is intensely hostile, gruff and highly critical of others—in order to protect himself from anxiety over being ridiculed or rejected.

People whose strong sexual feelings are repressed because they arouse high levels of state anxiety often display reaction formations. Consider the case of a young church minister whose normal sexual impulses arouse intense anxiety because he regards these feelings as sinful.[7] The minister tries to control both his anxiety and his unacceptable sexual feelings by a reaction formation. He vehemently denounces anything which might lead to sexual contact or attraction—holding hands, dancing, the use of lipstick—he even forbids boys and girls in his congregation to walk home from church together. The most fervent 'reformers' are often people who are strongly tempted by the 'evils' they seek to combat.

So psychological defence mechanisms can reduce state anxiety in two ways: by banishing threatening stimuli from the conscious mind; and by distorting a person's perception of potentially harmful situations so that they are considered less threatening. Defence mechanisms invest energy in internal psychological processes in order to reduce anxiety, while the underlying problems that caused the anxiety remain unchanged. To the extent that psychological defences protect a person from being overwhelmed by anxiety, they are helpful. But defence mechanisms are generally inefficient, and they become maladaptive if habitually used to reduce anxiety as an alternative to dealing effectively with the real source of stress.

Measuring A-State and A-Trait

A number of inventories, questionnaires and rating scales have been constructed to measure state and trait anxiety. People are asked to indicate whether a statement is generally true or false as it applies to them, or to rate themselves in terms of how accurately the statement describes their feelings. Brief self-report rating scales for measuring state and trait anxiety are provided in the tables on pages 76 and 77. You might like to try them on yourself.

It used to be called 'dicing with death'— do they do it because they fear it so much?

First, a word of warning about interpreting your results (and this applies equally to the rating scales on pages 76, 77, 89 and 116–17). Do not be alarmed by high scores: the scales are designed to give a very general idea of your response to stress, not to increase your anxiety! If you score high for all the scales, it would certainly do no harm for you to talk your feelings over with someone—preferably qualified. And do not omit to read the chapters on 'dealing with anxiety' on pages 90 and 104!

Before you begin, read the directions printed at the top of each table. Note that both the instructions and the rating categories for the state anxiety scale are different in important respects from those for the trait anxiety scale. Also, remember the definitions of state and trait anxiety: anxiety states are emotional reactions characterised by subjective, conscious feelings of tension, apprehension, nervousness and worry; trait anxiety refers to individual differences in anxiety proneness—that is, in the tendency to see the world as dangerous or threatening, and in the frequency that anxiety states are experienced.

The eight statements in the first table describe feelings that are related to *state anxiety* (A-State). In responding to these items, you must report the *intensity* of 'how you feel *right now*, that is, *at this moment*' by rating yourself on a four-point scale. For each item, circle the number under the column heading that best describes how you feel at the present time. After you have completed your ratings, you can determine your A-State score by simply adding up the eight numbers that you have circled.

The set of eight items in the second table describes feelings that are related to individual differences in *trait anxiety* (A-Trait). You should circle the number under the column heading that indicates how *frequently* you experience the symptoms of anxiety described by each item. To determine your A-Trait score, add the eight numbers that you have circled, just as you did in computing your A-State score. For both scales, your scores will vary between 8 (very low anxiety) and 32 (very high).

How do you compare?
In assessing your level of A-State, you were asked to report the degree to which you presently feel *calm* and *relaxed*; on the A-Trait scale you reported how frequently you generally feel *satisfied* and *secure*. These non-anxiety items are included to make the A-State and A-Trait scales more sensitive in measuring low levels of anxiety. Since these items indicate the absence of anxiety, they are scored in the opposite direction from items indicating the presence of anxiety: thus, feeling 'not at all' *calm* is scored '4' while feeling 'not at all' *tense* is scored '1'.

In order to compare your state and trait anxiety scores with those of other people, you will need to know something about *percentiles*. A percentile is a score that indicates how a particular person compares with a large number of people, called a *normative group*. Percentiles vary from 1 to 100. A person with a percentile score of 50 has an anxiety score that falls at the midpoint or *median* of the normative group, which means that 50 per cent of the people have lower scores. Similarly, people with scores that place them at the 25th percentile are more anxious than 75 per cent of the normative group; those with scores at the 95th percentile are more anxious than all but 5 per cent.

Now you are ready to consult the table on page 77 to determine how your anxiety scores compare with those of other people. To find out your percentile score on the A-State scale, compare your score with those reported in the table for a large group of males and females. If your score is actually recorded in the table, you can locate your percentile in the left hand column. For example, if you are male and your A-State score is 14, you rank at the 50th percentile. A female with an A-State score of 25 would fall at the 95th percentile.

If your A-Score does not appear in the table you can establish your approximate percentile by extrapolating from the scores that are reported. For example, suppose you want to know the percentile for a male with an A-State score of 11, which does not appear. Since 11 falls half way between 10 and 12, which have percentiles for males of 5 and 25 respectively, the percentile for a man with an A-State score of 11 would be about 15, which falls about half way between 5 and 25.

Now just imagine
Since the conditions under which you have just assessed your level of A-State were probably pretty relaxed, it is quite likely that you obtained a score of less than 15—which corresponds to a percentile below the median for the A-State scale. Now imagine that you are about to cross a busy street and suddenly discover that a speeding car you had not previously noticed is rapidly approaching you. Then read the A-State items in the first table on page 76 again and rate yourself according to how you believe you would feel immediately after you noticed your danger. In these imagined circumstances most people get A-State scores between 25 and 30, for which the corresponding percentiles are 95 to 100.

To find out your A-Trait percentile, compare your A-Trait score with those in the percentile table. The average A-Trait score is 15 for males and 16 for females; the A-Trait scores for most people fall somewhere between 12 and 21; which correspond approximately to percentiles of 20 and 80. Individuals who score below 12 are very low in anxiety proneness, and may be somewhat insensitive or unresponsive to other people. Persons with scores of 23 or higher are substantially more anxious than the average person and perhaps unduly sensitive to others.

Men with A-Trait scores of 24 or higher and women with scores of 26 or higher are much more anxious than the average person, and should seriously consider seeking help for their anxiety problems. If you obtained an A-Trait score of 24 or higher, this means that you 'often' or 'almost always' experience the feelings or thoughts described by the six items in the A-Trait table that indicate the presence of anxiety, and that you 'almost never' feel satisfied and secure.

State anxiety self-evaluation scale

Directions   Read each statement and then circle the number that indicates how you feel *right now*, that is, *at this moment*. There are no right or wrong answers. Do not spend too much time on any one statement, but give the answer which seems to describe your present feelings best. Add up the eight numbers you have circled to obtain your score.

	Not at all	Some-what	Moder-ately	Very much
I feel calm	4	3	2	1
I am tense	1	2	3	4
I feel upset	1	2	3	4
I feel frightened	1	2	3	4
I feel nervous	1	2	3	4
I am relaxed	4	3	2	1
I am worried	1	2	3	4
I feel confused	1	2	3	4

Having a clearly-defined costume can forestall one of the commonest stresses of more fluid societies— the sense of alienation.

Trait anxiety self-evaluation scale

Directions   Read each statement and then circle the appropriate number that indicates how you *generally* feel. There are no right or wrong answers. Do not spend too much time on any one statement, but give the answer which seems to describe how you *generally* feel. Add up the eight numbers you have circled to obtain your score.

	Almost never	Some-times	Often	Almost always
I feel nervous and restless	1	2	3	4
I feel satisfied with myself	4	3	2	1
I feel that difficulties are piling up so that I cannot overcome them	1	2	3	4
I feel like a failure	1	2	3	4
I have disturbing thoughts	1	2	3	4
I lack self-confidence	1	2	3	4
I feel secure	4	3	2	1
I worry too much over something that really does not matter	1	2	3	4

At one time he would have felt diffident, perhaps resentful, amid western self-confidence: now oil wealth has put the boot on the other foot.

Percentile ranks for state and trait anxiety scores

Percentile Ranks	State anxiety (A-State)		Trait anxiety (A-Trait)	
	Males	Females	Males	Females
95	21	25	23	25
75	17	17	18	20
50	14	15	15	16
25	12	12	13	13
5	10	10	10	10

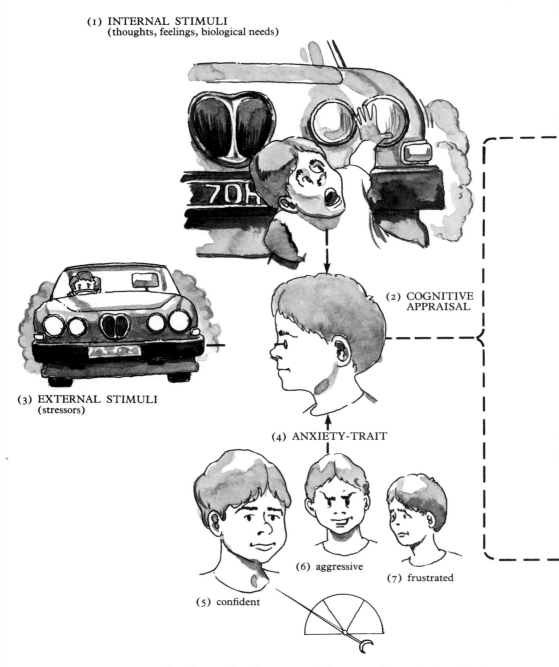

(1) INTERNAL STIMULI
(thoughts, feelings, biological needs)

(2) COGNITIVE APPRAISAL

(3) EXTERNAL STIMULI
(stressors)

(4) ANXIETY-TRAIT

(6) aggressive

(7) frustrated

(5) confident

A schematic diagram of the complex relationship between stressors, state and trait anxiety, and adjustment. The arousal of A-State involves a sequence of events in which an internal or external stimulus that is cognitively appraised as potentially dangerous or harmful evokes an A-State reaction. This reaction may then initiate a behaviour sequence designed to avoid the

(8) ANXIETY-STATE
(subjective feelings of
apprehension, anxiety expectation)

(11) BEHAVIOUR
('avoidance')

(9) DEFENCE
MECHANISM

(12) 'freezing'

(10) APPRAISED RESPONSE
TO THREATENING STIMULI

(13) 'escape (but into
the path of another car)'

danger, or activate internal psychological defences which alter
the cognitive appraisal of a situation. People who are high in
A-Trait tend to appraise social-evaluative situations as more
threatening than persons who are low in A-Trait. (Reprinted
with permission from C. D. Spielberger, *Anxiety and Behavior*,
1966.)

After the examination:
you see the same faces
of strain and fatigue
on soldiers after action.

80

6 Examination stress and achievement

We live in a test-conscious age, in which the lives of many people are greatly influenced by their test performance. To be accepted at a university and, especially, to be admitted to highly competitive professional training programmes like those in medicine and law, a student must have a very good academic record and, in addition, do well in difficult entrance examinations. It is therefore not altogether surprising that test anxiety is a pervasive problem among secondary school and university students. Indeed, the anxiety that some students experience during examinations is so disturbing that they are compelled to seek professional assistance to help them cope with its effects.

I first became concerned with the problems of examination stress and test anxiety in 1955 when I was associated with the Psychiatric Out-Patient Clinic at Duke University. The number of students attending the clinic seemed to increase during or immediately following university examination periods; and anxiety about academic performance was either the main symptom they wanted to discuss or an important background factor in their problem.

Students who sought help during the examination periods complained that anxiety made it difficult to study, and interfered with their thought processes during tests. Many students said they often 'knew' the answers to test questions but were not able to remember them because they 'blocked' or 'choked-up' during examinations. The level of achievement of these students did not reflect their intellectual ability, and it was apparent that test anxiety seriously interfered with their academic performance.[1]

A great deal has been learned about examination stress and test anxiety since these observations were made more than two decades ago. In this chapter, we will look at research on these common stressors and their effects on academic achievement. A rating scale is provided for measuring your own level of test anxiety and to see how you compare with other people.

Examination stress

In 1929, Walter B. Cannon observed that examination stress in humans seemed to produce the same biochemical changes that he observed in the fight-or-flight reactions of animals in stressful situations.[2] In Cannon's research, the pain inflicted on experimental animals caused an increase in blood sugar that sometimes resulted in glycosuria, a condition in which excess sugar in the bloodstream was passed in the urine. He believed that pain activated homeostatic mechanisms that released sugar into the bloodstream to energise the muscles and the brain for fight-or-flight reactions. Although examination stress was not physically painful, Cannon suspected that it might have similar effects because it was emotionally disturbing.

Cannon's views were supported by the results in several studies of examination stress.[3,4] In these investigations, students for whom there was no evidence of glycosuria on the day *before* a difficult examination, passed sugar in the urine immediately *after* the examination. In a related study, Cannon examined the urine of 25 members of the Harvard University football team immediately after the final and most exciting game of the season. Evidence of glycosuria was found for twelve members, including five substitutes who never even entered the game!

Taking part (above) or just watching, the excitement of games produces the same physiological responses.

The intense emotional reactions experienced during the examinations and the football game apparently contributed to the glycosuria exhibited by the students. This led Cannon to conclude that *emotional glycosuria* will result whenever a stressful situation produces an emotional state in which there is excess blood sugar that is not used up in fight-or-flight reactions.

Nearly 40 years ago, Charles H. Brown, a psychologist at the University of Chicago, called attention to the tragic consequences of examination stress and test anxiety.[5] Brown observed:

> In less than a year at one large University there were two suicides; one of these was definitely due to worry over an approaching examination and the other presumably was....
> These incidents show that students are taking their examinations more and more seriously, and that the emotional reactions of students before examinations is an important problem.

Alexander Luria, the renowned Russian psychophysiologist, observed that examination stress produces strong emotional reactions in some students while having relatively little effect on others.[6] Luria reported that 'unstable' students show speech and motor disturbances, and become excited and disorganised before and during examinations. The numbers involved may be very large world-wide: in Yugoslavia over 50 per cent of a large group of high school students were observed to experience severe test anxiety.[7] Considering how large a part examinations play in future 'success' in business, politics and the military, such findings must give cause for concern.

Anxiety and academic achievement

Most students see examination situations as threatening, and experience increases in state anxiety during tests. In general, predictably enough, the level of A-State is higher on difficult than on easy examinations. This means that very stiff examinations subject the candidate to two disadvantages—the intrinsic difficulty of the questions and a possibly distorting level of anxiety. For while a moderate increase in A-State during an examination can be helpful if it motivates the student to increase his effort and to focus his attention on the test materials, large increases in anxiety are likely to produce unrepresentatively poor test performances.

High trait anxiety is associated with poor achievement in primary, secondary and university students.[8,9] The adverse effects of trait anxiety on the academic performance of university students were explored in a study at Duke University in which trait anxiety was measured at the beginning of the term for more than 1,000 male students in introductory psychology courses.[10] The 20 per cent of students at each end of the anxiety scale were called the High (HA) and the Low (LA) Anxiety groups, and divided into five levels of intellectual ability from I (low) to V.

The grade-point average (GPA) for each student for the *single* term during which anxiety was measured was computed from official University records by awarding points from 4 (all As) to 0 (all Fs). The GPA's for high and low anxiety students are compared for each level of intellectual ability. The HA students received much lower grades than did the LA students in the broad middle range of ability, indicating that high levels of trait anxiety negatively affect academic performance. No differences were found in GPA's of HA and LA students of the lowest and highest scholastic aptitude: the highest got good grades irrespective of their anxiety level. On the other hand, the grades of the low aptitude students were uniformly low, irrespective of their anxiety level, indicating that their poor academic performance resulted primarily from their limited ability.

Levels of scholastic aptitude

Mean grade-point averages (GPA's) for high and low anxiety university students at five levels of scholastic aptitude. (Adapted from Spielberger, 1966)

To evaluate the long-term effects of anxiety on academic performance, a follow-up study was conducted three years later, by which time all the students should have graduated. However, about 15 per cent had not graduated and were no longer enrolled. The reasons for failure and the cumulative GPA's of the drop-outs were obtained from official University records. The results are shown in the table below.

Academic failure/drop-out rate for high (HA) and low (LA) anxious university students

Intellectual aptitude rating	HA Students		LA Students	
	Total number	Fail/drop-out No. per 100	Total number	Fail/drop-out No. per 100
V	22	2 9·1	30	3 10·0
IV	21	5 23·8	37	0 0·0
III	31	7 22·6	23	1 4·4
II	22	3 13·6	26	1 3·8
I	33	9 27·3	22	3 13·6
Total	129	26 20·2	138	8 5·8

In the follow-up study, academic failure was defined as: (1) having been dismissed from the University because of unsatisfactory academic performance, or (2) having left the University with a GPA too low for graduation. Both criteria were necessary because students who performed poorly were often allowed to withdraw for 'personal' reasons, so that the stigma of academic failure would not necessarily affect their being accepted by other colleges.

Of the HA students, more than 20 per cent were academic failures as compared to fewer than 6 per cent of the LA students. Anxiety clearly had a cumulative long-term influence on academic performance. This was especially true for HA students in the broad middle range of intellectual ability.

Anxiety contributes to the underachievement and/or academic failure of many potentially able students. If this is spotted early in their academic career and assistance is offered, the academic mortality rate of these students could be reduced. However, effective counselling of this sort must be based on a clear conception of the nature and measurement of test anxiety and its effects on academic achievement.

The nature of test anxiety

How does examination stress cause test anxiety? By what means does anxiety affect performance in test situations?

In the early 1950s, Seymour Sarason and George Mandler reported a series of studies in which they found that college students who were 'high test-anxious' did more poorly on intelligence tests than 'low test-anxious' students, especially when the tests were administered under stressful, ego-involving conditions. In contrast, high test-anxious students did relatively better under conditions in which stress was minimised, while low test-anxious students did more poorly under such conditions.[11]

Mandler and Sarason attributed the worsening of performance among test-anxious students to the arousal of 'feelings of inadequacy, helplessness, heightened somatic reactions, anticipation of punishment or loss of status and esteem, and implicit attempts at leaving the test situation'. Students with high test anxiety also tended to blame themselves for their poor performance, while low test-anxious students did not. High test-anxious students apparently respond to examination stress with intense emotional reactions and negative self-centred thoughts that impair performance, while those low in test anxiety react with increased motivation and concentration.[12]

Good preparation will not necessarily eliminate examination 'nerves'— but it can lessen guilty self-criticism, and allow concentration on performing well.

Worry and emotionality

It is now generally accepted that test anxiety consists of two major components: worry and emotionality. The worry component has been described as 'thoughts about the consequences of failure'.[13] The emotional component refers to the unpleasant feelings and physiological reactions that are evoked by examination stress. These two components seem to have different effects on test performance: the worry is associated with lowered performance in intellectual tasks, while emotionality appears not to be related to task performance.[14]

In examination situations, test-anxious students divide their attention between the demands of the test itself and activities like worry and self-criticism which are not relevant to the task at hand.[15] The latter distract the student from the requirements of the task and, thereby, contribute to poorer performance. Thus, under stress, high test-anxious persons divide their attention between 'self-relevant' and 'task-relevant' responses, while low test-anxious persons focus their undivided attention on the task. University of Washington psychologist Irwin G. Sarason describes the behaviour of test-anxious people in evaluative situations as follows:

> Whereas the less test-anxious person plunges into a task when he thinks he is being evaluated, the high test-anxious person plunges inward. He either neglects or misinterprets informational cues that may be readily available to him, or ... experiences attentional blocks.[16]

It seems clear from these findings that high test-anxious people are more prone than low test-anxious people to see examination situations as dangerous or threatening, and to become worried and anxious in such situations. Test anxiety may therefore be considered a *situation-specific* form of trait anxiety.[17]

The seminar, by making students familiar with the handling of learning against critical standards, acts as 'pre-stressing', so that tests hold fewer terrors for them.

Both the 'worry' and the 'emotionality' components of test anxiety appear to contribute to reducing the achievement of test-anxious students in intelligence tests and learning tasks: worrying thoughts distract the individual's attention from the task, and intense emotional reactions lead to mistakes and cause repression that blocks memory.

Measuring test anxiety

Test anxiety self-evaluation scale

Directions Read each statement and then circle the number under the column heading that best describes how you *generally* feel. There are no right or wrong answers. Do not spend too much time on any one statement, but give the answer which seems to describe how you generally feel. Add up the eight numbers you have circled to give your score.

	Almost never	Some-times	Often	Almost always
While taking examinations I have an uneasy, upset feeling	1	2	3	4
Thinking about the grade I may get in a course interferes with my work on tests	1	2	3	4
During exams I find myself thinking about whether I'll ever get through school	1	2	3	4
During tests I fell very tense	1	2	3	4
Thoughts of doing poorly interfere with my concentration on tests	1	2	3	4
I feel very panicky when I take an important test	1	2	3	4
I feel my heart beating very fast during important tests	1	2	3	4
During tests I find myself thinking about the consequences of failing	1	2	3	4

'Worry items' are in italics.

Percentiles for test anxiety scale and worry/emotionality subscales

Percentiles	Test anxiety		Worry		Emotionality	
	Male	Female	Male	Female	Male	Female
95	25	28	12	13	13	14
75	18	21	9	10	10	11
50	15	17	7	8	7	9
25	11	13	5	6	5	7
5	8	9	4	4	4	4

A rating scale for measuring test anxiety is provided in the table on page 88.[18] The eight statements in this table describe thoughts and feelings that people experience during tests. Four of these assess the tendency to worry and four describe the emotional reactions that people experience while taking tests.

To assess your own level of test anxiety, read each statement and then circle the number under the column that indicates how often you generally experience each of the symptoms of test anxiety. You can then compute your score by simply adding the eight numbers that you have circled. Test anxiety scores will vary between 8 (very low) and 32 (very high).

Four items in the table (printed in italics) make up the 'Worry' subscale. The remaining four constitute the 'Emotionality' subscale. You can compute your Worry and Emotionality scores by adding the four numbers that you circled for the items that correspond to each subscale.

The percentiles for scores on the Test Anxiety, Worry and Emotionality scales for large normative groups of males and females are shown in the table on page 88. For most people, the percentiles for test anxiety, and for worry and emotionality, will be comparable. For example, a female whose total score on the Test Anxiety scale is 21 (75th percentile) will probably obtain scores of 10 or 11 on the Worry and Emotionality subscales, which also correspond to the 75th percentile. However, many people respond to tests with increased emotionality, but relatively little worry. Less often, a person may worry a great deal on a test, yet score relatively low in emotionality. Worry during tests appears to be more detrimental to performance than emotionality.

After assessing your own level of test anxiety and its components, you should have a better understanding of the nature of test anxiety and how you compare with other people. In general, low scores in test anxiety are desirable. Therefore, if you obtained a score of 22 or higher on the Test Anxiety scale, and a Worry score of 12 or greater, your performance on tests is likely to be seriously impaired by anxiety. By contrast, students who score low in test worry, but who experience moderate increases in emotionality, seem to do best in most test situations.

7 Dealing with anxiety

Whenever a person regards a situation as threatening, he or she experiences an increase in anxiety as an emotional state. Anxiety states consist of unpleasant feelings of tension, apprehension, nervousness and worry which serve to alert people to the need to cope with stress. Since numerous stressors are encountered in daily life, everyone experiences anxiety states from time to time. These reactions are quite normal and generally adaptive because they mobilise the individual to avoid danger.

When intense A-State reactions occur in the absence of an objective danger, they indicate an underlying neurotic anxiety process. For example, intense anxiety states may be aroused in people with irrational fears and phobias by innocuous stimuli such as harmless animals or small enclosed places like closets or elevators. These stimuli trigger neurotic anxiety reactions because they are symbolically related to previous traumatic experiences that have been repressed.

Since neurotic anxiety reactions are aroused by *repressed* thoughts or feelings, one cannot deal directly with the source of threat. Psychological defence mechanisms are often used to reduce these unpleasant emotional states but, even when these mechanisms are successful, the underlying problems that caused the anxiety remain unchanged.

Responses to threat

Irrespective of whether the source of danger is internal or external, an A-State reaction is preceded by both a precipitating stimulus and the perception of threat. Thus:

$$\text{Internal or external stimulus} \rightarrow \text{Appraisal of threat} \rightarrow \text{A-State reaction}$$

Once aroused, an anxiety state may be eliminated in one of three way: by acting in such a way that the source of stress is avoided or the stress itself is lessened; by reappraising the stressor as less threatening; or by directly reducing the anxiety state itself.

When the world seems
too big, and you're made
to feel small . . .

Examples of each of these methods are described in the following sections of this chapter. In the final section, we consider various therapeutic approaches commonly used in the treatment of anxiety.

Eliminate or avoid danger

One of the most effective ways of reducing anxiety is to eliminate or avoid a stressor. The hunter who kills a rattlesnake that has invaded his campsite eliminates a source of real danger and will immediately experience a substantial reduction in his level of state anxiety. Similarly, the schoolboy who decides to take a longer route home in order to escape a beating from the local bully is avoiding a real danger.

'A substantial reduction in the level of state anxiety . . .'

People who work in stressful occupations can generally reduce their anxiety simply by taking a vacation or by changing jobs. Indeed, doctors often prescribe ocean voyages or restful holidays in pleasant surroundings for patients whose physical and emotional health is threatened by the pressures under which they live. However, eliminating or avoiding a stressor does not always reduce state anxiety. For example, after killing the rattlesnake, the hunter may lie awake all night dreading the appearance of the *next* deadly reptile which he expects to emerge from the shadows.

The capacity of human beings to remember traumatic past

experiences and to anticipate future dangers makes us highly susceptible and continually vulnerable to anxiety. The harried executive who goes on vacation may continue to worry about business matters, even though the source of his problem is thousands of miles away, and many combat veterans have recurring nightmares about their battlefield experiences for years after the hostilities have ended.

The stuff of recurring nightmares long after the war is over.

Take another look

There are, of course, many circumstances in which a danger cannot be either eliminated or avoided. An anxiety state can nevertheless be reduced if a stressful situation is reappraised as less threatening. It is the *appraisal of threat* rather than the objective danger itself that is the critical link in the stress-threat-anxiety chain.

There are many ways in which threat appraisals can be altered. If a situation changes or a person realises that it is not as dangerous as it initially appeared, a reduction in state anxiety will generally occur. But even a harmless or positive situation can precipitate a state anxiety reaction if it is seen as threatening. A student, worried about receiving a low grade in an important examination, nervously scans the list of grades and 'sees' a fail mark by his name. He begins to tremble and perspire as thoughts about the consequences of failure flash through his mind. Then he rechecks the examination results and discovers that he has mistaken his grade for that of another student with a similar name—his grade was actually a B, not an F. The student's state anxiety reaction resulted from his misperception of his grade, not from any real threat to his wellbeing.

Pretend it isn't there

If the source of danger is associated with repressed thoughts or feelings, then eliminating or avoiding these inaccessible internal stimuli may prove extremely difficult. In such cases, psychological defence mechanisms often come into play to reduce the anxiety states evoked by repressed thoughts or feelings. For example, repression and denial can be temporarily effective in alleviating anxiety by banishing threatening stimuli from awareness. State anxiety may also be reduced by rationalisation, intellectualisation and reaction formation, which allow a person to see a situation as less threatening. But defence mechanisms are generally inefficient and maladaptive because the underlying cause of the anxiety remains unchanged.

Tackling anxiety head on

There are two general approaches that people use to reduce the tension associated with anxiety states. One of these involves the use of chemical agents that diminish the anxiety symptoms themselves. The other is based on self-help techniques designed to produce a relaxed state of mind and body.

The chemical solution

The prevalence of the first of these approaches is illustrated by the fact that Americans annually consume more than 30 million pounds of aspirin (enough to take care of 20 billion headaches),

Talk, cigarettes and coffee-cups— a common, but not reliably effective, means of tackling anxiety.

and smoke more than 573 billion cigarettes.[1] The average American drinks more than four gallons of spirits and wine each year, plus 29·24 gallons of beer, and the annual rate of consumption of alcoholic beverages is increasing.[2] In recent years, the use of marijuana has also markedly increased, and there are many who advocate that it be legalised. While the reduction of anxiety is obviously not the only reason for the widespread consumption of aspirin, cigarettes, alcoholic beverages and marijuana, it is an important factor for many people.

Tranquillisers and sedatives are also widely used for relieving tension and anxiety. They account for about 20 per cent of all medications prescribed by physicians in the United States. The tremendous demand for these drugs has resulted in the annual production by American pharmaceutical companies alone of well over a million pounds of tranquillisers and about 900,000 pounds of barbiturates ('downers').[3]

Tranquillisers and barbiturates produce a variety of behavioural and emotional changes. In small amounts, they provide temporary relief from anxiety by reducing tension. However, increasing dosages produce sedation, then anaesthesia, and may even result in coma and death.

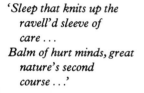

'Sleep that knits up the ravell'd sleeve of care ...
Balm of hurt minds, great nature's second course ...'

While the use of tranquillisers may be justified in helping people to deal with temporary emotional crises or emergencies, frequent and long-term use will generally lead to drug dependence. A drug-dependent person relies on chemical crutches for the relief of anxiety, rather than facing up to the stresses of life. Moreover, the continual use of drugs and alcohol to relieve

anxiety leads to increased tolerance, so that progressively larger doses of the substance are needed to produce the desired effects. This may result in extremely unpleasant withdrawal symptoms if the person tries to break the habit. Drug or alcohol addiction is a very high price to pay for what may have started as temporary relief from life stress and anxiety.

Help yourself

Self-help techniques designed to relax the mind and body generally provide a better means for reducing state anxiety than do drugs and alcohol. A conscious, deliberate effort to relax can often be effective in relieving tension and anxiety. Discussing a problem with a friend may also help relieve anxiety by bringing the source of stress out into the open, where it can be examined objectively.

Transcendental Meditation (TM) is an example of a mind-relaxing technique widely used to reduce state anxiety. Proponents of TM claim that more than 1·5 million people throughout the world currently use meditation to cope with stress.[4] The TM technique involves sitting quietly with eyes closed and allowing the mind to reflect without effort on a unique mental symbol, called a 'mantra', which is selected by the TM instructor to suit the meditator's temperament. Meditation exercises are typically practised in solitude for 15 to 20 minutes, twice each day.[5]

Meditation—more effective than it looks at relaxing the mind.

The goal of TM is to create a state of pleasant alertness and relaxation ('transcendental consciousness'), which is different

from normal wakefulness and sleep. In addition to relieving the symptoms of anxiety, there is some evidence that TM results in increased energy, greater inner control, better interpersonal relationships, and decreased drug abuse.[6] However, it has been suggested that simple relaxation training alone may have many of the same benefits as TM.[7] Indeed, techniques for relaxing the mind and the muscles are critical components in the psychological therapies that are used to treat anxiety disorders.

How others can help you

When an anxiety state is aroused by thoughts or feelings that are inaccessible because they have been repressed, eliminating or avoiding these unconscious sources of neurotic anxiety may prove extremely difficult. Since neurotic anxiety may need professional help, it is unfortunate that many of the people who

The drug path: only a crutch—when the trip is over the crippling anxiety is still there.

suffer from it are reluctant to seek treatment from psychiatrists or psychologists for their emotional problems because of the stigma associated with being labelled 'mentally ill'. They prefer instead to depend upon crutches such as drugs and alcohol to alleviate their anxiety; or they attempt to reduce anxiety by investing a great deal of energy in psychological defence mechanisms.

Since the founding of psychoanalysis by Sigmund Freud at the beginning of this century, more and more people have sought out psychological treatment to help them cope with mental and emotional problems. In fact, there has been such a proliferation of new forms of psychological treatment over the past two decades that today it can be difficult for troubled people to choose the type of treatment best suited to alleviating their problems.

Most people who seek psychological treatment suffer from a disturbed state of mind in which anxiety and depression are the most prominent symptoms. These symptoms are generally associated with low self-esteem and unsatisfactory personal relationships. Therefore the goals of most types of psychological treatment are to reduce anxiety and depression, to improve the patient's self-respect, and to help him to establish more satisfying relationships with other people.

Psychological treatments can be classified in many different ways. From the standpoint of relieving anxiety, psychological treatments can be divided into two broad categories: firstly, treatments designed to reduce state anxiety directly; and

Training in bio-feedback techniques can help to control the worst effects of stress.

secondly, treatments that attempt to modify a person's appraisal of anxiety-arousing situations so that they will seem to be less threatening.

Systematic desensitisation

Systematic desensitisation is a form of psychological treatment that is especially effective in reducing anxiety associated with irrational fears and phobias. For some people, travelling by plane, talking over the telephone, or simply walking to the local shopping centre, can be extremely threatening. Others become intensely anxious when they encounter or think about relatively harmless animals like mice or spiders. Irrational reactions to stimuli or situations that are *not* objectively dangerous reflect an underlying neurotic anxiety process.

Systematic desensitisation and related psychological treatment techniques such as *reciprocal inhibition* and *counterconditioning* were popularised by Joseph Wolpe in the late 1950s.[8] These treatments work by pairing a state of physical and mental relaxation with an anxiety-arousing object or scene imagined by the patient. The treatment rationale is that being relaxed is incompatible with the tension and worry that are experienced in intense states of anxiety.

Relaxation classes and counselling sessions are now more easily available to the anxious.

A step-by-step approach

The first step in systematic desensitisation is to evaluate the patient's problem so that the behaviours that are to be modified can be identified. This can usually be accomplished in a few intensive interviews in which the therapist determines the circumstances that cause the patient to feel anxious. Most people can describe specific situations in which they feel intense anxiety and discomfort, and similar circumstances in which they experience milder reactions. For example, a test-anxious student may report experiencing: (1) mild anxiety when it is announced in class that a test will be given in two weeks; (2) a moderate amount of anxiety while studying at home the day before the test; and (3) extremely high anxiety while actually taking the test. Thus, through careful inquiry, the therapist constructs an *anxiety hierarchy*, which consists of a graded list of situations that evoke mild to intense A-State reactions.

The next step in systematic desensitisation is to train the patient in deep muscle relaxation. While comfortably seated, the patient carries out exercises to help him become more aware of the muscular tension that usually accompanies the high levels of state anxiety associated with irrational fears and phobias. Through training in the contraction ('tensing') and relaxing of different muscle groups, the patient learns how to relax the muscles in all parts of his body.

Military training uses 'stress inoculation' to guard against soldiers collapsing under pressure. Recruits are put through it all beforehand.

All in the mind's eye

After the patient has mastered the muscle relaxation techniques, the desensitisation proper begins. As the patient relaxes, he is asked to imagine, as vividly as possible, the least threatening scene from the anxiety hierarchy which has been constructed. A test-anxious student might be asked to imagine that his instructor has just announced that a test will be given in two weeks. If the student experiences any anxiety, he is instructed to discontinue visualising the scene and to concentrate on relaxing. But if no anxiety is aroused, the student is instructed to visualise a more threatening scene—to imagine that it is the day before the test and he is studying for it. This procedure will be repeated until the student is able to relax even when he is imagining the most stressful scene in the hierarchy.

As systematic desensitisation progresses, a patient should be able to imagine situations that previously evoked intense anxiety reactions without experiencing any discomfort, including eventually the most threatening scene in the hierarchy. When this point in treatment is reached, the patient has become *desensitised* to his irrational fear and should be free from anxiety when feared objects or situations are actually encountered in real life. Wolpe and others who have used desensitisation techniques claim that 90 percent of their patients recover or show marked improvement.[9]

Reappraising the threat

Techniques of mind control used by Buddhist monks have been found effective by westerners.

Rational Emotive Therapy (RET) is based on the premise that an *appraisal of threat* is the critical link in the stress–threat–anxiety chain. It helps patients to reduce anxiety by teaching them to modify appraisals of threat that are based on *irrational beliefs*. This form of psychological treatment was developed by the American psychologist, Albert Ellis,[10] at about the same time that Wolpe introduced systematic desensitisation.

How rational emotive therapy works

The goal of RET is to convince the patient that his neurotic anxiety is caused by his faulty perception or irrational beliefs about stressful events, rather than by the events themselves. In order to get better, the patient must learn how to 'challenge' these beliefs so that he can replace them with more realistic, rational appraisals. By eliminating the irrational beliefs that lead to unfounded appraisals of threat, the emotional turmoil that results from 'crazy thinking' can be alleviated.

Fellow-refugees from violent homes: for both of them, 'a trouble shared is a trouble halved'.

In treating a student with test anxiety, an RET therapist would point out that the student's fears about the consequences of failure are in fact exaggerated. His anxiety is therefore caused by his irrational beliefs rather than by the objective danger. Furthermore, by viewing a bad grade as a disaster, the student's appraisal of threat intensifies his test anxiety, which further undermines his performance.

The triumph of logic

In challenging the student's belief that it would be 'just awful' or 'catastrophic' to do poorly in a test, an RET therapist would insist that the student had grossly exaggerated the realistic consequences of his academic performance. The therapist would agree that receiving a low grade might indeed be unfortunate and might even require the student to repeat the course, or even to change his career plans. But he would emphasise that receiving a low grade does not make him a worthless person, and he would help the student to evaluate rationally the consequences of his academic performance. He might also point out that many students who change careers are happier in a different field than the one they chose originally.

In vigorously disputing a patient's illogical ideas, the RET therapist teaches him to monitor his own thoughts so that he can identify, analyse and challenge those irrational beliefs that contribute to his emotional problems.[11] RET is successful when irrational thoughts and beliefs are eliminated. The patient is then free to focus his attention on logical, effective ways of dealing with stressful life events and getting more satisfaction out of living.

Psychoanalysis—the key to painful memories
Like RET, psychoanalysis and psychoanalytic therapy are concerned with altering the appraisals of threat that lead to neurotic anxiety reactions. However, in contrast to RET—which probes the patient's overt irrational beliefs—psychoanalysis investigates the underlying causes of the patient's emotional problems. Using the method of *free association*, the analyst helps his patient to probe his unconscious mind in order to discover repressed traumatic childhood experiences that continue to influence thoughts, feelings and behaviour. The goal of psychoanalysis is to give the patient *insight* into how repressed feelings associated with these childhood events contribute to his present problems.

The type of psychological treatment that will be most effective will depend upon the nature and severity of the problem, the individual's intellectual capacity, and his willingness to invest the time and energy needed to bring about a beneficial change. A critical factor in the success of any treatment will be the competence and experience of the therapist. Therefore, before seeking treatment, one should make extensive inquiries about available treatments. The problem of choosing a suitable therapist will be considered in greater detail in the final chapter.

8   Living with stress and anxiety

Stress, as we have seen, refers to a complex transaction between a person and his environment in which external forces or pressure (stressors) are linked to state anxiety by the perception of threat.

The internal processes activated in stress transactions prepare people for 'fight-or-flight'. In this book, we have concentrated on the arousal of state anxiety and associated flight reactions in situations that are seen as potentially harmful.

But an event or situation that frightens one person may simply anger or irritate others who see the situation as frustrating and this will depend on the stressor, the individual's ability, coping skills and personality traits, and his previous experience with similar situations. Situations that frustrate people generally provoke anger, which serves to energise fight reactions. But frustrating situations may also evoke anxiety in people who anticipate that they will be punished if their anger is expressed. Such people tend to experience anxiety states more often than other people do and are thus high in trait anxiety. High trait anxiety, combined with the inability to express anger even when it is appropriate, is characteristic of neurotic persons.

Not all a bad thing

Stress can have positive as well as negative effects. Everyone needs at least a little excitement. People become bored when the level of stress is extremely low, and some will actively seek out stressful situations such as riding a roller coaster, watching horror films, skiing or mountaineering. Others take their need for excitement to greater lengths, and pursue careers as test pilots, racing drivers or steeplechase jockeys. These activities may seem stimulating and challenging to the people who engage in them, but others may avoid them as simply too dangerous or frightening. The type of jobs people hold, and the leisure activities they choose, reflect important individual differences in how stressors are seen by different people.

*A little voluntary
stress may be essential
to keep people healthy.*

In sheltered societies, the demand for a little excitement may be met in the fairground.

The complexity of modern life practically guarantees that nearly everyone will be confronted periodically with dangerous or embarrassing situations that cause them anxiety. There are no universal laws telling us how to handle our stress transactions, because people differ so greatly in the traits they inherit and in their life experiences. However, some general guidelines are suggested below that may help you to cope more effectively with life's crises as well as with the ordinary run of irritations and annoyances.

Stress and anxiety can be overwhelming, causing us to feel miserable, desperate, and helpless. If these intensely unpleasant feelings and the stressors that seem to cause them persist, it may be wise to seek assistance from others and the final section of this chapter suggests ways of finding professional help in cases of unmanageable stress and debilitating anxiety.

Guidelines for living with stress and anxiety

An important first step is to become more aware of the experience of anxiety as an emotional state. Once anxiety states can be reliably identified, the next step is to watch when they happen and analyse the situations that produce them. In that way, you can discover the sources of threat. This means carefully evaluating the events associated with anxiety states; and also analysing your thoughts and ideas at the time.

The third step is to ask yourself whether your anxiety reactions are appropriate to the physical or psychological dangers which provoked them. Look carefully at the ways in which you try to eliminate, avoid or cope with sources of undesirable stress.

The most effective means of dealing with maladaptive anxiety is to understand fully the problem and then to develop the coping skills that will enable you to reduce the threat. Step four is to examine your resources for coping with anxiety.

The fifth and final step is to examine your level of anxiety proneness and see if you can identify psychological defences for controlling anxiety. If you find that you are high in trait anxiety and make excessive use of maladaptive defences, then unmanageable stress and debilitating anxiety are clearly serious problems for you, and you may need professional help.

Know when you feel anxious

Anxiety as an emotional state consists of a unique combination of unpleasant thoughts and feelings as well as internal physiological changes associated with activation of the autonomic nervous system (see Chapter 3). Anxiety states vary in intensity. Apprehension, tension, and nervousness are experienced at low to moderate levels of state anxiety. But high levels of state anxiety are characterised by overwhelming fear, sometimes even by panic behaviour. Moderate to high levels of state anxiety may also be reflected in restlessness, trembling, shortness of breath, sweaty palms and muscular tics and twitches. With increasing state anxiety, there is also increased heart rate, a rise in blood pressure, rapid breathing and muscular tension.

*Fire ... fifteen floors up!
The beginnings of
panic fear that
can prompt irrational
escape attempts ending
in needless tragedy.*

The particular psychophysiological and behavioural changes associated with high state anxiety differ, however, from person to person. For example, the young woman examination candidate (see Chapter 1) perspired, trembled, and felt nauseous and dizzy as the papers for the university entrance examination were being distributed, while the young motor mechanic had a headache and felt a 'knot' in his stomach, with dryness of the throat and rapid heartbeat as he waited for his job interview.

When you are faced with a stressful situation, you can estimate your level of state anxiety by examining your subjective feelings and monitoring your physiological symptoms and behavioural changes. You can also use self-report ratings like the State Anxiety Self-Evaluation Scale provided in Chapter 5 to assess your state anxiety level at a particular time, and to compare differences in the intensity of your anxiety reactions to different stressors.

Identify stressors that cause you to feel anxious
Beginning with the trauma of birth itself, many different physical and psychological stressors are encountered in the course of human growth and development. Major life crises like the death

Backside rostrum;
and wayside pulpit.

of a spouse, divorce or a jail sentence are extremely stressful. But while they have similar effects on people, in terms of the amount of readjustment required to cope with them, the same stressor may affect different people in different ways. The amount of anxiety aroused depends on an individual's interpretation of an event as threatening. In the appraisal of threat, the objective magnitude of the danger will certainly be an important factor. However, threat appraisals are also influenced by the thoughts and memories stimulated by a stressor, and by a person's coping skills and previous experience with similar circumstances.

In order to discover the stressors that cause you anxiety, you need to examine the circumstances in which your anxiety reactions occur. When confronted with environmental stressors that are potentially harmful—for example, having a tooth out, driving in bad weather, or walking through a neighbourhood in which street crimes frequently occur—the source of threat will be readily apparent. In such cases, an increase in state anxiety is a normal, natural reaction that will arouse and motivate you to take whatever precautions are required to avoid, eliminate, or minimise the danger.

However, when you feel anxious in situations in which there is *no* crisis or obvious external physical danger, it is difficult to identify the stressor. By analysing your own thoughts and feelings in these situations—and especially the nature of your relationships with other people—you may be able to discover why you feel threatened. For example many people are afraid of failure, have exaggerated ideas about the effects of poor performance and worry about how they are evaluated by others. These are all important sources of psychological stress.

The face of worry.

Analyse your stress transactions: is your anxiety appropriate?

Once you have learned to recognise your anxious feelings and can identify the physical and psychological stressors that cause them, you can analyse your stress transactions. Are they proportionate to the real danger? By monitoring your anxiety and the situations in which it occurs you may also be able to indentify the sources of stress that cause you to experience debilitating anxiety.

In practice, of course it can be difficult to decide whether the intensity of an anxiety state *is* appropriate to the magnitude of the objective danger. One way of doing this would be to compare your anxiety reactions to different stressors with those of other people. However, since high levels of state anxiety may distort the accuracy of your perceptions, it may be helpful to discuss your anxiety reactions and the stressors that cause them with a trusted friend who can help you to be more objective.

Confiding in a friend can help put your worry in perspective ...

Intense anxiety in situations in which there is little objective danger usually indicates an underlying neurotic anxiety process. The source of the danger in such neurotic anxiety lies in repressed thoughts and feelings rather than in external stressors. Irrational fears and phobias result from neurotic anxiety: they are evoked by objects or situations that are, in fact, harmless. Fortunately, many neurotic anxiety reactions can be effectively eliminated or reduced by psychological treatment.

Examine your resources for coping with anxiety

After you have identified the circumstances that cause maladaptive anxiety reactions, you can consider ways of eliminating or avoiding undesirable stressors, or minimising their impact. How you do this will depend upon your personal resources for coping with stress and anxiety.

It is often possible to eliminate or minimise external dangers simply by avoiding them or taking safety precautions. For example, people who work in demanding occupations can reduce or avoid stress by taking a restful vacation or changing jobs. But the constant pressures encountered in stressful environments can have cumulative effects. In these circumstances (like the straw that broke the camel's back) even a minor stressor can lead to intense anxiety reactions. Thus, simply avoiding the physical presence of external stressors may not lead to reductions in anxiety, because human beings have the capacity to remember traumatic past experiences and to anticipate their happening again.

When a stressor cannot be avoided, the most direct and effective way of dealing with anxiety is to do something to eliminate or reduce the actual danger. The anxiety caused by day-to-day irritations can be reduced by developing effective habits for responding to routine demands in a timely and orderly manner. Even major life crises can be anticipated and will generally cause less anxiety and fewer problems if one prepares for them by developing contingency plans.

... and even in a major crisis of the spirit, friendly support will not be wasted.

When a person has a toothache, taking aspirin may provide temporary relief from the pain. But anxiety about the cause of the toothache will persist, and one must eventually consult a dentist to remedy the problem. Simply making an appointment with a dentist may be sufficient to alleviate the anxiety. Indeed, facing up to the problem may even reduce the pain, since high anxiety tends to make us more sensitive to painful stimuli.

Two aspects of reassurance— the formal solace of religion . . .

The successful management of stress transactions will depend upon the total resources available to a person for coping with a particular stressor. For example, suppose an instructor in a difficult course announces that an examination will be given the following week. The best way a student can cope with the anxiety aroused by the announcement is to study the assigned lessons. The effectiveness of this coping behaviour will depend on factors like his study skills, his general knowledge of the subject and the demands of other activities that compete for his time.

. . . and the comforting protection of force.

Many people who are especially vulnerable to stress lack confidence in their social skills—hence the popularity of courses designed to 'win friends and influence people'[1]. Special programmes in personality development, public speaking, and sensitivity and assertiveness training help people to reduce anxiety by developing their personal resources for coping with stressful social situations.

Evaluate your trait anxiety; test your defences

People who are high in trait anxiety tend to view the world as more dangerous or threatening than do persons who are low in A-Trait. Consequently, they are more vulnerable to stress and often feel tense, nervous, restless, insecure and dissatisfied with themselves. They are also more prone to neurotic anxiety reactions to dangers, in which derivatives of repressed thoughts or memories erupt into consciousness, and raise the level of state anxiety substantially beyond what would be warranted by the objective danger. Neurotic anxiety is always maladaptive because it mobilises the individual to adjust to the repressed memories of past dangers that no longer exist.

In their efforts to cope with stress, high A-Trait people make excessive use of psychological defence mechanisms. Some also turn to drugs and alcohol to relieve their anxiety. But while tranquillisers and sedatives give temporary relief from anxiety, and are often effective in helping people cope with emergencies and emotional crises, they do not deal directly with the source of stress (and they may lead to dependence, too).

Like tranquillisers and sedatives, psychological defence mechanisms can be useful in cases of overwhelming anxiety. But defences such as repression, denial and rationalisation are

'What King Canute was really trying to do . . .' but you need to be low in trait anxiety to sit through the history lesson!

generally inefficient because the energy invested in them could be used for more productive purposes. Moreover the underlying causes of the anxiety remain unchanged and effective coping behaviours fail to develop.

So it is important for you to understand your own level of trait anxiety and the extent to which you rely on various defence mechanisms. By comparing your score on the Trait Anxiety Self-Evaluation Scale provided in Chapter 5 with the scores in the table on page 77 you can get some idea of whether you are trait-anxious or not. If you find that your trait anxiety is very high (above the 95th percentile), and there are many situations in which you feel incapacitated by anxiety, you should seriously consider obtaining professional help. This is especially true if you seem to make excessive use of drugs, alcohol or psychological defences for controlling stress and anxiety.

Seeking professional help with anxiety problems

When chronic anxiety makes you feel miserable during the day and disturbs your sleep at night, it is time to seek professional help. Like making an appointment with your dentist when you have a toothache, seeking psychological treatment for unmanageable stress and debilitating anxiety is an important first step in facing up to these problems.

'... I spake of most disastrous chances, Of moving accidents by flood and field ... This to hear Would Desdemona seriously incline.'
(Shakespeare: Othello)

Only a small proportion of those who need psychological treatment actually seek it. Some avoid treatment because they fear they will be labelled 'mentally ill', others because this might be interpreted by family and friends as a sign of personal weakness or because they refuse to admit, even to themselves, that they are unable to cope with life stress.

Two additional obstacles to psychological treatment are its cost in terms of both time and money, and the difficulty of choosing a qualified therapist. Psychological treatment generally requires a great deal of time and personal commitment as well as a substantial financial sacrifice, especially if long term treatment is required.

In choosing a suitable therapist, one must have some knowledge of the type of treatment that would be most beneficial, and then be able to locate a person who is qualified to provide this treatment. Finding a suitable and qualified therapist may be a problem for people with limited financial resources, and for those who do not live in a large metropolitan area. So it is not surprising that many people who need professional psychological assistance do not seek it until they are overwhelmed with unmanageable stress and debilitating anxiety.

There are a number of books devoted entirely to helping people sort out the multitude of factors that must be considered in seeking psychological treatment.[2,3] But your family doctor or minister can usually refer you to a competent counsellor or psychotherapist, and you can also consult the directors of local mental health agencies. Tremendous strides have been made in recent years by the psychological helping professions and it is now much easier to obtain professional help in coping with stress and anxiety.

Life change and stress

Thomas H. Holmes and his colleagues at the University of Washington School of Medicine have developed a scale for measuring the seriousness of changes in American people's lives and related their scores to their chances of becoming ill. The Survey of Recent Experiences (SRE) consists of 43 different life changes that have been scaled in *Life Change Units* (LCU) for the degree of adaptation they require.

Americans are thought to run the risk of developing a major illness in the next two years if they total more than 300 LCU points. If appropriate, calculate your own LCU rating.

Survey of Recent Experiences

Life Events	*Life Change Units*
Death of spouse	100
Divorce	73
Marital separation	65
Jail term	63
Death of close family member	63
Personal injury or illness	53
Marriage	50
Fired at work	47
Marital reconciliation	45
Retirement	45
Change in health of family member	44
Pregnancy	40
Sex difficulties	39
Gain of new family member	39
Business readjustment	39
Change in financial state	38
Death of close friend	37
Change to different line of work	36
Change in number of arguments with spouse	35
Mortgage over $10,000	31
Foreclosure of mortgage or loan	30
Change in responsibilities at work	29
Son or daughter leaving home	29
Trouble with in-laws	29
Outstanding personal achievement	28
Wife begins or stops work	26

(continued)

Life Events	Life Change Units
Begin or end school	26
Change in living conditions	25
Revision of personal habits	24
Trouble with boss	23
Change in work hours or conditions	20
Change in residence	20
Change in schools	20
Change in recreation	19
Change in church activities	19
Change in social activities	18
Mortgage or loan less than $10,000	17
Change in sleeping habits	16
Change in number of family get-togethers	15
Change in eating habits	15
Vacation	13
Christmas	12
Minor violations of the law	11

References

1   Stress and strain

1. Selye, H. *Stress without Distress*. Philadelphia: J. B. Lippincott, 1974.
2. *Time*, March 31, 1961, p. 44.
3. Hinkle. L. E. The concept of 'stress' in the biological and social sciences. *International Journal of Psychiatry in Medicine*, 1974, *5*, 355–357.
4. Bueche, F. *Principles of Physics*. New York: McGraw-Hill, 1977, p. 195.
5. Osler, W. 'The Lumleian lectures on angina pectoris', *The Lancet*, 1910, *1*, 698.
6. Spielberger, C. D. Anxiety as an emotional state. In C. D. Spielberger (Ed.), *Anxiety: Current Trends in Theory and Research (Vol. 1)*. New York: Academic Press, 1972.
7. Ibid.
8. Lazarus, R. S. *Psychological Stress and the Coping Process*. New York: McGraw-Hill, 1966.

2   Sources of stress

1. Rank, O. *The Trauma of Birth*. New York: Robert Brunner, 1952.
2. McDonald, R. L. The role of emotional factors in obstetric complications: A review. *Psychosomatic Medicine*, 1968, *30*, 222–237.
3. Spielberger, C. D., & Jacobs, G. A. Stress and anxiety during pregnancy and labour. In L. Zichella and P. Pancheri (Eds.), *Clinical Psychoneuroendocrinology in Reproduction*. New York: Academic Press, 1978.
4. Gorsuch, R. L., & Key, M. K. Abnormalities of pregnancy as a function of anxiety and life stress. *Psychosomatic Medicine*, 1974, *36*, 352–362.
5. Edwards, K. R., & Jones, M. R. Personality changes related to pregnancy and obstetric complications. *Proceedings of the 78th Annual Convention of the American Psychological Association*, 1970, 341–342.
6. Kagan, J. Personality, behaviour and temperament. In F. Falkner (Ed.), *Human Development*. Philadelphia: W. B. Saunders, 1966.
7. Sikes, S. M. *The relationship of anxiety and reading in first grade children*. Unpublished Master's Thesis, University of South Florida, Tampa, 1978.
8. Papay, J. P., Costello, R. J., Hedl, J. J., Jr., & Spielberger, C. D. Effects of trait and state anxiety on the performance of elementary school children in traditional and individual multiage classrooms. *Journal of Educational Psychology*, 1975, *67*, 840–846.
9. Seidenburg, R. *Corporate Wives—Corporate Casualties*. New York: American Management Associations, 1973.
10. Nelson, Z. P., & Smith, W. E. The law enforcement profession: An incident of high suicide. *Omega*, 1970, *1*, 243–244.
11. Cobb, S. & Rose, R. M. Hypertension, peptic ulcer and diabetes in Air Traffic Controllers. *Journal of the American Medical Association*, 1973, *224*, 489–492.
12. Glass, D. C., & Singer, J. E. *Urban stress: Experiments on noise and social stressors*. New York: Academic Press, 1972.

13. Stokols, D., Novaco, R. W., Stokols, J., & Campbell, J. Traffic congestion, Type-A behavior and stress. *Journal of Applied Psychology*, 1979, in press.
14. Holmes, T. H., & Rahe, R. H. The Social Readjustment Rating Scale. *Journal of Psychosomatic Research*, 1967, *11*, 213–218.
15. Harman, D. K., Masuda, M., & Holmes, T. H. The Social Readjustment Rating Scale: A cross-cultural study of Western Europeans and Americans. *Journal of Psychosomatic Research*, 1970, *14*, 391–400.

3   Feeling threatened

1. Lazarus, R. S. *op. cit.*, 1966.
2. Cannon, W. B. *Bodily Changes in Pain, Hunger, Fear, and Rage.* New York: Appleton, 1929.
3. Selye, H. *The Stress of Life (Revised Edition).* New York: McGraw-Hill, 1956.
4. Mason, J. W. A historical view of the stress field. *Journal of Human Stress*, 1975, *1*, 23–36.
5. Spielberger, C. D. *op. cit.*, 1972.
6. Spielberger, C. D. *op. cit.*, 1972.
7. Spielberger, C. D., Gorsuch, R. L., Lushene, R. E., *Manual for the State-Trait Anxiety Inventory.* Palo Alto Calif.: Consulting Psychologists Press, 1970.
8. Lazarus, R. E. *op. cit.*, 1966.

4   Fear and anxiety

1. Cohen, J. Personality Dynamics. Chicago: Rand McNally 1969.
2. Kritzeck, J. Philosophers of anxiety. *Commonweal*, 1955/56, *63*, 572–574.
3. Darwin, C. *Expression of Emotions in Man and Animals.* Chicago: University of Chicago Press, 1965 (originally published, 1872).
4. May, R. *The Meaning of Anxiety (Revised Edition).* New York: W. W. Norton, 1977.
5. Freud, S. *The Problem of Anxiety.* New York: W. W. Norton, 1936.
6. Ibid., p. 85.
7. Freud, S. *New Introductory Lectures in Psychoanalysis.* New York: W. W. Norton, 1933, p. 133.
8. Freud, S. *Collected Papers (Vol. 1).* London: Hogarth Press, 1924.
9. Freud, S. *op. cit.*, 1936, pp. 69–70.
10. Matsuda, M., & Holmes, T. H. *op. cit.*, 1967.
11. Spielberger, C. D. *op. cit.*, 1972.

5   Patterns of adjustment

1. Spielberger, C. D. *op. cit.*, 1972.
2. Spielberger, C. D. *op. cit.*, 1972.
3. Perdue, O. and Spielberger, C. D. Anxiety and the perception of punishment. *Mental Hygiene*, 1966, *50*, 390–397.
4. Freud, A. *The Ego and the Mechanisms of Defense.* New York: International Universities Press, 1946.
5. Bourne, P. G. *Men, Stress and Vietnam.* Boston: Little, Brown and Company, 1970.
6. Hodges, W. F. & Spielberger, C. D. The effects of threat of shock and heart rates for subjects who differ in manifest anxiety and fear of shock. *Psychophysiology*, 1966, *2*, 287–294.
7. Morgan, J. J. B. *How to Keep a Sound Mind* (Rev. ed.). New York: MacMillan, 1946.

6   Examination stress and achievement

1. Spielberger, C. D. The effects of manifest anxiety on the academic achievement of college students. *Mental Hygiene*, 1962, *46*, 420–426.

2. Cannon, W. B. *op. cit.*, 1929.

3. Folin, O., Denis, W., & Smillie, W. G. Some other variations on emotional glycosuria in man. *Journal of Biological Chemistry*, 1914, *17*, 519–520.

4. Cannon, W. B. *op. cit.*, 1929.

5. Brown, C. H. Emotional reactions before examinations: III. Interrelations. *Journal of Psychology*, 1938, *5*, 27–31.

6. Luria, A. R. The nature of human conflicts (translated by W. H. Gantt). New York: Liverlight, 1932.

7. Eric, L., Melcer, T., Kovacevic, N., Stevanovic, L., & Drulovic, R. Test anxiety and its features. *Anali*, 1973, *5*, 71–80.

8. Spielberger, C. D., Gorsuch, R. L., & Lushene, R. E. *op. cit.*, 1970.

9. Spielberger, C. D. *State-Trait Anxiety Inventory for Children: Preliminary Manual.* Palo Alto: Consulting Psychologists Press, 1973.

10. Spielberger, C. D. *op. cit.*, 1962.

11. Mandler, G., & Sarason, S. B. A study of anxiety and learning. *Journal of Abnormal and Social Psychology*, 1952, *47*, 166–173.

12. Sarason, S. B., & Mandler G. Some correlates of test anxiety. *The Journal of Abnormal and Social Psychology*, 1952, *57*, 810–817.

13. Liebert, R. M., & Morris, L. W. Cognitive and emotional components of test anxiety: A distinction and some initial data. *Psychological Reports*, 1967, *20*, 975–978.

14. Morris, L. W., & Liebert, R. M. The effects of anxiety on timed and untimed intelligence tests: Another look. *Journal of Consulting and Clinical Psychology*, 1969, *33*, 240–244.

15. Wine, J. Test anxiety and direction of attention. *Psychological Bulletin*, 1971, *76*, 92–104.

16. Sarason, I. G. Experimental approaches to test anxiety: Attention and the uses of information. In C. D. Spielberger (Ed.), *Anxiety: Current Trends in Theory and Research* (Vol. 2). New York: Academic Press, 1972.

17. Spielberger, C. D., Gonzalez, H. P., Taylor, C., Algaze, B., & Anton, W. D. Examination stress and test anxiety. In C. D. Spielberger & I. G. Sarason (Eds.), *Stress and Anxiety*, (Vol. 5). New York: Hemisphere/Wiley, 1978.

18. Spielberger, C. D., Gonzalez, H. P., Taylor, C. J., Anton, W. D., Algaze, B., & Ross, G. R. *Preliminary Test Manual for the Test Anxiety Inventory.* Palo Alto: Consulting Psychologists Press, 1979.

7 Dealing with anxiety

1. Henslin, J. M. Toward a national drug policy. In *Problems of Drug Dependence: 1975 Proceedings of the Thirty-Seventh Annual Scientific Meeting, Committee on Problems of Drug Dependence.* Washington: National Academy of Sciences, 1975, p. 1158.

2. Ibid, p. 1166.

3. Ibid, p. 1157.

4. Kanellakos, D. P. Transcendental consciousness: Expanded awareness as a means of preventing and eliminating the effects of stress. In C. D. Spielberger and I. G. Sarason (Eds.), *Stress and Anxiety* (Vol. 5). Washington: Hemisphere/Wiley, 1978.

5. Bloomfield, H. H. Applications of the transcendental meditation program to psychiatry. In V. Binder, A. Binder and B. Rimland (Eds.), *Modern Therapies.* Englewood Cliffs, N. J.: Prentice-Hall, 1976.

6. Orme-Johnson, D. W., & Farrow, J. T. (Eds.). *Scientific Research on the Transcendental Meditation Program: Collected Papers* (Vol. 1), Rheinweiller, German Federal Republic: MERU Press, and Livingston Manor, N.Y.: MIU Press, 1976.

7. Benson, H. *The Relaxation Response.* New York: William Morrow, 1975.
8. Wolpe, J. *Psychotherapy by Reciprocal Inhibition.* Stanford, Calif: Stanford University Press, 1958.
9. Strupp, H. H. *Psychotherapy and Modification of Abnormal Behavior.* New York: McGraw-Hill, 1971.
10. Ellis, A. *Reason and Emotion in Psychotherapy.* New York: L. Stuart, 1962.
11. Ellis, A., & Grieger, R. (Eds.). *Handbook of Rational-Emotive Therapy.* New York: Springer, 1977.

8 Living with stress and anxiety

1. Carnegie, D. *How to Win Friends and Influence People.* New York: Simon and Schuster, 1936.
2. Ehrenberg, O., & Ehrenberg, M. *The Psychotherapy Maze: A Consumers Guide to the Ins and Outs of Therapy.* New York: Holt, Rinehart, and Winston, 1977.
3. Kovel, J. *A Complete Guide to Therapy: From Psychoanalysis to Behavior Modification.* New York: Pantheon Books, 1976.

Suggested further reading

1. Lazarus, R. S. *Psychological Stress and the Coping Process*. New York: McGraw-Hill, 1966.
2. Levitt, E. E. *The Psychology of Anxiety*. New York: Bobbs-Merrill, 1967.
3. May, R. *The Meaning of Anxiety* (*Revised Edition*). New York: W. W. Norton, 1977.
4. Schoonmaker, A. N. *Anxiety and the Executive*. Washington: American Management Association.
5. Selye, H. *The Stress of Life* (*Revised Edition*). New York: McGraw-Hill, 1956.
6. Selye, H. *Stress without Distress*. Philadelphia: J. B. Lippincott, 1974.
7. Sheehy, G. *Passages: Predictable Crises of Adult Life*. New York: Bantam Books, 1976.
8. Spielberger, C. D. (Ed.), *Anxiety and Behaviour*. New York: Academic Press, 1966.
9. Spielberger, C. D. (Ed.), *Anxiety: Current Trends in Theory and Research* (*Vol. 1*). New York: Academic Press, 1972.

Index

Photo credits

Michael Abrahams—19; Ian Barry—6; Herbert Bishko—8 (*bottom*), 45 (*top*); By courtesy of British Airways—9, 16 (*top*); Ron Chapman—34, 38, 50, 59, 66, 94, 106, 114; Colin Curwood—99 (*bottom*); Vera Etzion—27; John Garrett—52; Geoslides—76 (*2*); Henry Grant—95; Richard and Sally Greenhill—67, 110, 111; Neil Gulliver—7 (*right*); Simon Harper—108 (*right*); Israel Sun—5, (Israel Simionsk) 33 (*top*), 69 (*top*), 72; Sheelah Latham—10, 63; Lisa Mackson—7 (*left*), 12, 80, 82 (*2*), 86, 87, 105, 112 (*top*); Monitin (illustrator: Michael Kushka)—28–29; Mothercare—20; Moshe Orbach—45 (*bottom*); PAF—21; Popperfoto—32 (*left*), 51, 64 (*left*), 70, 107; Rex Features—8 (*top*), 13, 16, 24, 37, 43, 55, 60 (*2*), 61 (*2*), 64 (*right*), 68, 93, 102, 108 (*left*), 109, (Arepi) 101, (Agence Dalmas) 53 (*left*), (David McEnery) 31, 91, (Omnia Press) 26, (Sipa Press) 15, 22, 33 (*bottom*), 40, 48, 53 (*right*), 69 (*bottom*), 100, 112 (*bottom*), (Vizo) 97, (Frank Wilcox) 44 (*top*), 73, (George Zygmund) 65; Anat Rotem—32 (*right*); Phil Sheldon—39 (*2*); Barry Sheridan—99 (*top*); Michael Slatford—98; Homer Sykes—71, 77, 96, 113; Syndication International—30; John Walmsley—92.

Illustrators: *Oxford Illustrators Ltd.*—41, 42, 54, 56, 57, 78–79, 84; *Diana Sherman*—44 (*bottom*).